THE DIVORCE
DIET

Other Works by Renee Lear

Circumstantial

Times Three

My Friend Gavin

THE DIVORCE
DIET

RENEE LEAR

Copyright © 2019 by Renee Lear.

ISBN Softcover   978-1-950580-72-9

All rights reserved. No part of this book may be reproduced or transmitted in any form or by any means, electronic or mechanical, including photocopying, recording, or by any information storage and retrieval system without express written permission from the author, except in the case of brief quotations embodied in critical reviews and certain other non-commercial uses permitted by copyright law.

Printed in the United States of America.

To order additional copies of this book, contact:
Bookwhip
1-855-339-3589
https://www.bookwhip.com

Contents

- The Decision Making Process 1
- Spending Habits 8
    - o "Unnecessary" Spending Habits 8
    - o "Necessary" Spending Habits 10
        - Groceries 10
        - Clothing 16
        - Transportation & Gas 18
        - Shelter 22
        - Credit Cards 28
        - Savings 28
        - Student Loans 31
- Personal Finance Workbook 33
    - o Current Monthly Expenses 33
    - o Modified Monthly Expenses 34
- Setting Your Budget 38
- How Your Credit Affects Your Lifestyle 41
    - Credit Scores 41
    - How do credit scores impact your life? 43
    - How long does it take to repair your credit? 44
    - Building or Re-Building Credit 51
    - Collections 54
    - Credit Repair Companies 57
    - Bankruptcy 59
    - o Debt Repayment Plan 60

- ➤ Personal Goals 62
    - o Setting and Obtaining Personal Goals 69
    - o MSI's or Multiple Sources of Income 70
    - o The "Process" 72
- ➤ Lifestyle Changes 75
    - o Changes with Friends & Family 78
    - o Do What You Love 81
    - o "Indoor Camping" 82
    - o Spiritual Motivation 82
    - o Manifest Greatness 85
    - o Being "Selfish" 86
- ➤ Patience & Focus 91

Conclusion 93

The Decision Making Process

Merriam-Webster defines ***divorce*** as a noun to mean "the action or instance of legally dissolving marriage", and as a verb to mean "to legally dissolve one's marriage; to end marriage with one's spouse by divorce".

To those of us who have been through divorce, we simply call it, "The End". Although it is the end of a relationship, it is just the beginning of the change in your lifestyle. Going from two people that make decisions together (or maybe not, since divorce is happening), to simply standing alone as an individual. More importantly (to some of us) is going from two incomes down to one.

Many people speaking about the concept of divorce will say "I can't afford to get divorced". This doesn't typically mean that they can't afford the divorce attorney, or the process of divorce, it means that they can't "afford" to maintain their current lifestyle with only one income.

Merriam-Webster defines ***diet*** as a noun to mean "a regimen of eating and drinking sparingly so as to reduce one's weight", and as a verb to mean "to cause to eat and drink sparingly or according to prescribed rules".

For those of us going through a divorce or dealing with the aftermath of a divorce, your finances and possibly your body had to go on a serious "diet". After being divorced for about four months I had lost around 20 pounds. People who hadn't seen me in a while would say, "You look great, did you go on a diet?" I would laugh and say, "Yes, I went on The Divorce Diet. It's great!" Like any diet, it may be uncomfortable at first, but once you embrace it, it could possibly be the best decision you've ever made.

Maintaining your current lifestyle is important to most people. You're accustomed to living a certain way, your spending habits are relatively predictable, you know exactly what your rent/mortgage, car payments, utilities, groceries, and outside spending habits will be each month. Most partners share in these expenses and therefore it is almost impossible to maintain your current lifestyle when one income leaves the building.

When children are involved this concept becomes the most concerning. It's hard enough on kids to have their parents parting ways, but when this means that they have to leave their home, possibly relocate which means a change in friends and schools, and change their spending habits for clothing and entertainment, most children can become extremely distraught by this.

In America in particular, we are defined by our social class. What you wear, what you drive, where you live, and the amount of technical devices that you own tend to define your personality. One motivational speaker I listen to said, "We have so many names of other people on our clothing and accessories that we forget our own name" - JO. Sad but true for some of us.

So…you clung to your marriage so that you could avoid the financial catastrophes that would come about from also divorcing that other income. However, life has come to the point where you decide to move forward, and you've made the decision to get divorced, or maybe that decision was made for you by your partner. Either way, now it's time to get serious about your financial situation and what is to come.

Your new financial situation is going to put you into one of three categories:

1. UNCOMFORTABLE = this will be a small lifestyle change that will involve a modification of spending habits. You may not be able to get your $5 coffee every morning; buy new clothes every weekend; pay to get your nails and hair done; go on those hunting and fishing trips with your buddies; go on the yearly girl's trip with your friends; eat out every day for lunch; or eat out on a regular basis.

   While these things will be "uncomfortable", they will not be a complete change in lifestyle, they will simply affect your social lifestyle. Your home and auto will not need to be modified, only your basic spending habits.

2. STRUGGLE = the loss of the secondary income will cause you to have to downgrade your home, car, or both. In this scenario you've already acknowledged the fact that you will be "uncomfortable" and having to deal with everything that comes with that category, and in addition you don't have the income to maintain your current living status. Downgrading from a home to an apartment, or from an apartment that has multiple bedrooms to a smaller place can be an emotional struggle as well as a financial struggle. Additionally, that great car that you love so much that has the $500 monthly payment suddenly has to go unless you want to live in your car. Unless that car comes with a shower, this is obviously not the best scenario, and therefore downsizing your vehicle is necessary to keep your finances under control.

   Depending on what you do for a living, who your friends are, and how emotionally attached you are to your vehicle, this could also be a serious emotional struggle.

3. DEVASTATION = the complete loss of your home, your car, and/or your assets. The loss of the secondary income will cause you to be unable to have a place of your own to live, and/or you will not be able to keep a vehicle at all. This category represents "leaving with the clothes on your back", literally.

   Being unable to afford a home or place to live on your own income means that you will have to live with friends, family, sublet from strangers, or be forced to live in a shelter until you are able to regain control of your finances.

   The loss of a vehicle means that you are suddenly at the mercy of your area's public transportation system; asking friends, family, or co-workers for rides; or hiring a driving company such as a Taxi,

Uber, or Lyft to get you where you need to go. This category is the hardest to deal with and will be the most difficult to recover from.

I was unfortunately in this category when I made the decision to leave my ex. I'm guessing that doesn't make you feel any better at this particular point in time, however, I was able to pull myself from the depths of darkness of the devastation category back up to having MSI's (Multiple Sources of Income) and was able to purchase a home within 3.5 years, and by myself I might add! It wasn't easy, and it took serious dedication to personal goals, however I did it and so can you. The only person that can ever stop you from achieving anything you want, is yourself. If you remember that, then nothing can stop you.

Most of you already have an idea which category you are going to fall into. The Workbook section of this book will help you to break down your finances to determine what changes will need to be made and will ultimately determine exactly which category you fall into. Once you've crunched the numbers, you will know where you stand which will allow you to start making a plan for the recovery process.

If your divorce isn't final yet and you're making preliminary decisions, let me chime in right now and say this, DO NOT KEEP ANY JOINT ASSETS!! I can tell you that a devasting thing for a Realtor is to have a great client with excellent credit, however they are unable to qualify for a new home because they let their ex-spouse keep their prior residence, and they don't have a debt to income ratio that will qualify them for a new purchase. Or they make plenty of money, but their credit is now blown because the ex-spouse that wanted to "keep the house" or "keep the car" didn't make payments on time or defaulted on the payments which directly affects everyone on the Note/Lien regardless of what is stated in a Divorce Decree.

I'm going to write this next part in all caps, bold, and underlined to get my point clearly across…**<u>YOU ARE RESPONSIBLE FOR ALL ITEMS ON YOUR CREDIT REPORT AND THOSE DEBTS WILL COUNT AGAINST YOUR DEBT TO INCOME RATIO REGARDLESS OF WHAT YOUR DIVORCE DECREE STATES!!!</u>**

What that means is that if you have a house in both of your names, and your vehicles are in both of your names, then even after the divorce is final your personal "debt" that new creditors will be showing that you are responsible for will still be the home and both cars, regardless of where you live, what you drive, and what a Judge said each person is responsible for. It is rare for a creditor to disregard items on your credit report that are active and show you as a "Joint" applicant/debtor aka a person responsible for that debt.

In addition to that, let me add this in the same manner… **IF YOUR EX-SPOUSE WAS AWARDED THE PROPERTY, VEHICLE OR CREDIT CARDS IN THE DIVORCE AND THEY MAKE LATE PAYMENTS OR DEFAULT ON PAYMENTS THIS WILL DIRECTLY AFFECT YOUR CREDIT REGARDLESS OF WHAT YOUR DIVORCE DECREE STATES!!!**

Even if your divorce decree states that only one party is financially responsible for the debt, the judge can't make a creditor or lien holder force anyone to refinance, therefore the original Note or Lien stays in place, and any payments made, good or bad, will affect both parties that are responsible for the debt. Sure, you can always submit a copy of your decree to the creditor or lien holder and to the credit bureaus, but it's simply an attachment to the file. It is rare to get a letter saying, "Oh sorry about those derogatory comments on your credit report, we'll remove those right away!"

If you are actually able to find creditors or finance companies that will honor the stipulations of the divorce decree, then that is amazing! If all companies would honor divorce decrees then our credit scores and financial statements would look much better than they do, but most companies will hold to the primary Note that was put in place for the debt until it is paid off, or until another Note takes its place (e.g.: refinance).

In most cases your divorce decree is irrelevant to lien holders, it's simply a Civil Case document that helps authorities determine whose is whose, in the event that matters verge on the domestic dispute or criminal side of things. If you try to tell the police that you're going to sleep on the couch, regardless of the fact that the house was awarded to your ex-spouse, simply because the house payments are still showing up on your credit report, you're going to have a problem. In these circumstances the decree will come into effect, and only in reference to who is allowed to physically possess the items.

When it comes to how those things are getting paid for, that is not for law enforcement, that is the creditor's world, and creditors literally do not care that you decided to no longer be partners. What they care about is getting the money that they are owed. They don't care who it comes from, as long as it comes in full and in the timeframe agreed upon when you both went into debt in the first place. If not, it will be reported to the credit bureaus for all parties related to the debt. .

The only time it is a good idea to let someone "keep" a joint asset is if they can get that asset refinanced into their name only which will pay off the "Joint" account and create a new "Individual" account. If they can't refinance, then they can't afford it on their own anyway and need to let it go.

If you have a joint property, SELL IT, or let the party that wants to remain in the property refinance the property into their name only. If both of your names are on your vehicles, TRADE THEM or REFINANCE THEM! Outstanding credit card balances in play? ROLL OVER that balance into a new card in one person's name only or split it onto two new separate cards or accounts!

Here's a news flash for those of you that think you're going to be able to make the house payment because you'll be getting that "child support money", if those payments aren't garnished from the other parent's wages, and they're not willing to give it to you in a timely manner, good luck with that! Unfortunately, some people think that child support money will come just like social security money, except that your ex-spouse isn't a division of a government institution, and therefore, you shouldn't expect to sustain your lifestyle on that money. If your ex-spouse loses their job, guess what? Those payments can get cut in half, or be put on hold all together, then what?

The best advice I can give you is to rely on your own income or your own means of generating money because when you put your faith in another person, you are ultimately at the mercy of that person, and in my experience, that's not a reliable or pleasant place to be. For those of you that have no income, I was there myself when I left my ex, being a full-time student doesn't pay the bills. We will cover how to get your finances under your own control later using MSI (Multiple Sources of Income) examples in the Personal Goals section.

Many of you won't want to make those hard changes that we're talking about because you feel like you're entitled to keep something that you can't afford on your own. Know that holding onto things you can't afford is only going to prolong the issue. It's the same as plugging a boat with a cork, or a bullet wound with a cotton ball, eventually you're going to sink, bleed out, or both.

Let's get started analyzing your budget so that you can determine where you stand.

Spending Habits

Spending money, the great American past time! Most Americans find the making of money to be a tedious undertaking, however they sure do love to spend it. Currently I live in Colorado, so I'm blessed to have a multitude of places to "get out of the house" for free, however most people that live in cities or places where outdoor recreation is minimal, tend to view going to the mall or going out shopping to be a weekend recreational activity.

Breaking down and analyzing your spending habits is the best way to get a good idea as to whether or not the modification of the way you spend money can help you keep your home or car instead of having to downsize either of those two important areas.

What type of consumer are you? We're all consumers so the question is, what, when, and how do you consume? How much do you spend money on items that are "unnecessary", and how much do you spend on "necessary" items?

"Unnecessary" Spending Habits

If you spend money on items that are "unnecessary", your spending habits could put you into one of these categories:

- Impulse shopper = You didn't intend to spend money however you saw something you just "had to have", and therefore spent the money to obtain it. You went into the huge grocery/department store for some milk and bread, but you managed to gravitate to the clothing section and bought items that were not on your list and were not the focus of your trip to the store. Instead of spending $5 you spent $50. Although it wasn't planned, you're all good because you got items you would have eventually needed...

- Bulk shopper = You have that membership, so you've got to use it. You shop in bulk and pay $20 for 10 items that you only really need one of, but you had to because you saved money by buying in bulk. Checking out you spend $200+ for bulk items that you really only needed one of and could have paid $50 or less for by buying single individual units instead of multiple bulk items. It wasn't absolutely necessary to buy that many, but the apocalypse could happen at any time and at least you'll be prepared to never run out of soap or paper towels.
- Coupon shopper = You buy items that you have coupons for with the justification that it would be more expensive without the coupon. Yes, you're saving money, but did you really need the item/s you're purchasing? Could you have bought a store brand instead that was $1 less than the name brand that you have a $0.50 coupon for? Was the item even on your grocery list before you saw the coupon??
- Sale shopper = You don't necessarily "need" new clothes, but you got that department store flier in the mail and they're having a sale and you could save 50% or more!! You run off to the store and spend $100 that wasn't in your budget, but you justify it because those items would have been $275 if they weren't on sale. So, instead of acknowledging the fact that you spent $100 you didn't need to spend, you instead tell yourself that you "saved" $175.
- Eating out = Look at your bank account and add up all the money you have spent eating out for lunches and for dinners. Lunches can typically be $50 per week as the average for lunch is $10. This makes eating out for lunches $200 per month. Eating out for dinners is typically $15 per person plus a tip so the average for a dinner is $35 - $70 depending on the size of your family. Eating out only once a weekend at $50 per dinner also equals $200 per month. Therefore,

an average person can spend up to $400 per month just by eating out for lunch and only once a weekend.

The circumstances above represent times that you spend money when it isn't "absolutely necessary". By monitoring your spending habits in these areas, you will be surprised at the amount of money you can keep in your budget. Most people have serious denial issues when it comes to spending money that was "unnecessary". What I would like for you to do right now, is to log into your bank account and look at the places that you've spent money in the last month. Now open your calculator app and punch in every dollar that you spent that was unrelated to paying bills…

How'd you do? Either you have a great handle on your spending habits, you don't have the extra money to shop in those manners, or you just figured out that you would have $100 - $300+ more a month if you get those categories under control.

"Necessary" Spending Habits

Now let's talk about "necessary spending". These consist of spending money for shelter, car, insurance, utilities, phone, internet (for most of us this is a necessity these days), groceries, gas, and clothing. Let's take a look at your spending habits in these areas to determine if you are able to save money.

Groceries

This is the best area to analyze first because while food is a necessity, most of us tend to overspend in this area. All of us, regardless of social class, have to eat and therefore have to shop for groceries. What are you currently spending on groceries each week? If you can't immediately answer that question then your spending habits in this area tend to vary, which isn't optimal for budgeting money for your trips to the grocery store.

When I was married our grocery budget was $400 a week. My ex-husband was a 6'3" construction worker that could eat a serious amount of food. We had three kids at home who also had good appetites and who expected to have an abundance of snacks, and their favorite thing to drink in the fridge. I will say with my work schedule and family schedule I wanted to buy everything for the week at once so that price also included whatever toiletries or laundry detergent, etc. that was needed for the week. I also cooked dinner every night so that included all meals for the week. $400 sounds like a lot but some of you with the same family size can attest to the fact that I did some serious budgeting just to get to that amount.

Are you thinking that you have minimal money for groceries and that you're unable to determine how you're even going to pay for food? I understand and I've been there. I went from having $400 a week for groceries to dealing with having $20 to last for two weeks. Not an exaggeration or a joke. What did I do? I bought boxes of pasta that cost $1, cans of sauce that costs $1, a loaf of bread that costs $1, and a jar of peanut butter that costs $3, and we drank water from the tap.

We're from Texas so yes, we are serious carnivores and I could eat steak for breakfast, lunch, and dinner. Obviously, meat was one of the first things I had to cut out of the budget, and the only protein we were getting at that time was peanut butter. We're actually still alive to talk about it and write about it, so no matter how hard it gets, I promise you can get through it.

Let's get into your grocery budget and attempt to find areas where you can save. If you do some simple modifications to your current shopping habits, you might be able to maintain your food budget without having to go on too much of a "diet".

> **Drinks** – What amount do you spend each week on drinks alone? If you have an athlete in the house do you buy Sports drinks? And if you do, do you buy the individual bottles so that they can grab one and go? Do you buy soda in cans by the 12 pack or by the case? Do you buy bottled water? Do you buy gallons of tea or lemonade pre-made? Do you buy individual 1 serving coffee refills instead of buying a full container of coffee grounds?
>   o Now, add up all the money that you spend on drinks alone, then multiply that by 4 if you do this each week. This is the amount you spend per month on drinks alone. For some of us that amount could be equivalent to your cell phone bill, half of your electric bill, exceed your water bill, etc. If you seriously need this money for your bills, then you need to look

at substitutions so that you can allocate more money to your bills and less to your grocery budget.

- o What's the best alternative to save money in this area? If you live in an area where tap water is safe to drink then you could buy a half gallon or a gallon pitcher and begin making tea, lemonade, or other drinks that have a cost of the tea bags or drink mix, and a bag of sugar only.

  If your tap water isn't the best, then look into a water service. In most areas you can get a water delivery service that will still allow you to save money by having the water delivered in a large container then using it to make the drinks you want. Most grocery stores also have a station where you can fill up 2.5 gallon or 5 gallon containers on site, which will save you the delivery service fee.

  Your biggest push back in this area is going to come from your children. I don't know about you, but I am guilty of spoiling my children when it comes to getting everyone what they want from the grocery store. Divorce is difficult on many levels so unfortunately you may have to show them your budget breakdown and give them the reality check that if they want electricity, then they're going to have to deal with drinking water instead of soda…

➤ **Snacks** – I'm guessing that if you buy snacks then you buy them in a box where each snack inside that box is individually packaged. If so, then a lot of what you are paying for is packaging, aka trash.

   I'm not a fan of social media, however the one app I can't live without is Pinterest! It doesn't matter what type of snacks you buy I'm guessing that you can find a food hack that replicates those snacks at a fraction of the cost. Buy a box of baggies and make your snacks then "package" them yourself by putting them in the individual baggies.

   If you have access to the internet, then you have access to a multitude of ideas that will help you keep spending low and satisfaction high. You might actually have fun while you're at it!

➤ **Frozen Foods** – This falls into the same category as Snacks because if you're buying frozen foods you're also buying them in freezer proof packaging, which is a lot of the cost. Now, if you're buying the budget food items that only cost a dollar or two, then most likely you won't be able to replicate those, however if you're buying family meals, waffles, pancakes, "meals in a bag" and things of that nature, then you should be able to find a recipe that will help you make the same thing for a fraction of the cost. If you make an abundance, then you can also buy freezer bags and freeze them that way.

- o If you are in the habit of buying frozen lunches, then price out the cost of taking your own salad or additional options that may save you money in this area during the week.
- o Many of you with small children may buy bags of frozen chicken nuggets and French fries. A big bag of chicken nuggets typically costs around $10 and a 1lb bag of fries costs $3. Watch for sales on chicken breasts and you can get a large package for $6-7, which will make double, if not triple the amount in the pre-packaged bag. Put flour in a container with your favorite seasonings, which could be as simple as salt and pepper, whip up an egg and do the rotation of flour, egg, flour, then fry or bake depending on the recipe you go with. A 5lb bag of Russet potatoes typically costs $3, so you're getting 4x the amount of potatoes by taking the time to break those down into fries yourself. These can also be either fried or baked depending on your personal preference.

For meals in a bag and other things that you like to buy, search for comparable recipes and see if you can save any money by making those yourself as well.

➢ **Proteins** – Now is the time to watch those sale ads!! The meals I make each week are fully dictated by what proteins happen to be on sale that week. As I said previously, we're from Texas so I am very familiar with what each cut of beef costs. That is, until we moved to Colorado and I went to the store to buy some chopped steak and a roast!

When I had a limited budget in Texas we would have Chicken Fried Steak, aka Southern Fried Steak, which is chopped steak breaded and fried.

In Texas you can get 4 "steaks" for around $5. I was standing in the Colorado grocery store with a limited budget staring at the 4 pieces of chopped steak that had a price tag of $12.50. I apparently looked so distraught and stood there for so long that the meat manager came out and asked if he could help me. I said, "I'm just trying to figure out why chopped steak, meat that really isn't worthy of having 'steak' in its name, costs over $12." He laughed and said, "You're from Texas aren't you?"

He pointed to a roast that cost $25 and asked me how much a roast of that size would be in Texas, to which I replied no more than $15. I should add that we're from Amarillo, which is considered by some to be the beef capital of the United States. Now that we don't live there, when we drive back to visit and are about 15 minutes into the Texas state line my son will always say, "What's that smell Mommy?" So, I can assure you that there is never a shortage of beef where we come from.

The meat manager was nice enough to ask me what I would normally have paid for the chopped steak and he put a "Manager's Discount" sticker on it and sold it to me for $6 all while saying that was a one-time nicety due to my beef shock. He also said that he had just done the same thing for a man from Oregon for a fresh side of salmon he had been looking at. His exact quote, "You need to realize that you're not in Texas anymore and he's not by the ocean anymore." True!! The price of protein is determined by the area you live in.

The good news is, if you're a fan of chicken, then good for you! The price of chicken seems to be equivalent in most areas that I've lived and if you only buy it when it's on sale then you should be able to become a chicken connoisseur with the amount of chicken recipes that are out there. Many stores will have chicken drums or chicken thighs for $5 or less and at least once a month my favorite store here will do a "Buy One Get One" sale.

One of my favorite things about chicken is that you can make it taste several different ways simply by changing up what you put on it. BBQ sauce comes in many different flavors, there are a ton of amazing Asian sauces to choose from, and by simply using salt, pepper, and buying a fresh lemon to squeeze over it, you can create some fantastic dishes.

Depending on where you live the price of fish will vary. In Texas and Colorado both, fish can be pricey so I watch for sales on frozen fish. Fresh fish, may or may not be so "fresh", depending on where it came from and how long it's been sitting there if you live in a state that is land locked.

Tilapia is one of the least expensive types of fish to buy. While most people that eat an abundance of fish will tell you that Tilapia is a "dirty fish", it is served in most restaurants across the US and it can be breaded, grilled, baked, and made in many different ways that can change up the flavor.

If your first instinct is to say, "I don't like fish", then challenge yourself to find a recipe that looks good and give it a try. Ironically last night I made Alaskan Salmon, lemon butter rice, and roasted asparagus. My mother, 24-year-old son, and granddaughter recently moved in with me and while I've always cooked dinner, I never used to cook any type of fish, so they've had to get used to my new recipes. Our previous diet was beef, beef, beef, pork, and chicken! They both thought that they didn't like fish and my mother had never tried salmon prior to living with me.

So…how much do you think I spent on that dinner? Sounds great right? If you go to a nice restaurant and purchase a salmon dish, you're most likely going to pay anywhere from $15 to $20+ per person or meal depending on the restaurant.

Well, my grocery store had frozen Alaskan Salmon filet on sale for $7.99 (normal cost = $15.99); I used 3 cups of Jasmine rice (my favorite) and an entire bag of that rice = $3 so I would say I used about $1.50 of rice; then the grocery store also had asparagus on sale for $2.99 for a bundle and I bought 2 because my 16-year-old can eat an entire bundle himself; and I bought 1 fresh lemon which was $0.50. Total cost of the salmon, rice, asparagus dish that fed 3 adults, a 16-year-old, my granddaughter, and even a small piece went to my dog Odin who is also spoiled = $15.97 which is the price of feeding only 1 person if you let a restaurant do the cooking for you.

If you've never cooked before and all of these ideas seem to be daunting, I hope that you can start to enjoy the process of cooking with the motivation that it will save you money.

I'm not much of a shopper so cutting out spending in most areas was easy for me to do. However, I LOVE food! I spent 9.5 years in real estate and one of the most wonderful things about that industry is that we have meetings while eating! If you love to eat out and hate or dislike cooking, then this can be one of the most challenging parts of The Divorce Diet.

Not having money to eat out or to eat what you want can add to the psychological issues you are already having because many of us find comfort in food, therefore when that food is taken away it adds to our distress.

Again, make a list of the foods that you love to order when you go out to eat, then search for recipes to try to make that same dish at home. You may have to wait for the protein to go on sale to be able to afford to make it, but you could surprise yourself by making something amazing and you might actually begin to love cooking.

If you're thinking that you could be a great cook if only you had the right seasonings, let me tell you, my staple seasonings are season salt, garlic powder, and pepper! When I cook for people, they're always telling me how wonderful my seasoning is, and I rarely use anything but those three items. If you can afford more herbs and spices, then great, that will only enhance your flavor profiles, but if you can't, then stick to those three and you'll be good to go!

Grocery apps are wonderful tools to help you keep from exceeding your grocery budget! You can sit in the comfort of your home and create your list, add things to your cart, and then modify as necessary to ensure that you don't exceed your budget. You can view the Weekly Ads to determine what is on sale and you can look at the Coupon list to determine if those can help you with the items already on your list. The "Pick-Up" fee is typically $5 but that is a small price to pay to keep from exceeding your budget at the register and having to deal with embarrassment or anxiety related to overspending.

Clothing

Once again, regardless of your social class, we all have to wear clothes, and even if you made your clothes yourself you would still have to buy the material, so all of us typically spend money on clothing. The question is, how much do you spend on clothing? Do you only buy clothes when the seasons change, when something doesn't fit anymore, when school starts, or do you buy clothes on a monthly basis?

Previously we talked about buying clothes in an "unnecessary" setting, however, let's talk about when buying clothes is "necessary". When it is necessary to buy new clothing then you should absolutely look for those sale ads! Keep an eye out for clothing stores that are "Going Out of Business", and any other scenario where you could save money.

The last thing that many of you want to hear is to shop at a Thrift Store. In your mind buying used clothing is something that you simply refuse to do, for multiple reasons that you've convinced yourself make sense. Since the point of getting new clothes is for them to be in good condition, or "new", okay I won't say that a quick fix is to thrift shop. However, as many of you that used to have a healthy budget for shopping can attest to, if you thrift shop at a location that is close to an upper scale neighborhood, many of the clothes in the building still have their original department store tags! Some people donate clothing to thrift stores because they've run out of closet space, not because the clothes are worn out. Remember that statement about recreational shopping?? One can't possibly keep up with their favorite recreational activity if one is out of closet space!

> **Seasonal Shopping-** If it's about to be winter and all of your previous winter clothes no longer fit, then of course it would be necessary to buy clothes to keep you warm, BUT if your winter clothes from last year are still intact and still fit, then buying new winter clothes isn't "necessary". As adults we can typically wear the same clothes year after year, the only "need" for new clothes is psychological.

Right now, I'm wearing a sweatshirt that I've owned since I was 8 years old and I'm currently 43. Needless to say, all of my family members have been tired of seeing me in this same sweatshirt year after year, (sometimes day after day in the winter), however it still fits and it's my favorite thing to wear around the house! It's a college sweatshirt and I actually attended the University for over a year before we moved, so at least at one point it matched what I was doing. I have about five other perfectly good sweatshirts hanging in the closet, but what can I say, I prefer this one. I literally didn't "need" any of the others, and I didn't buy the others. They were given to me in an attempt to get me to stop wearing this one. At this point it's vintage so I'm not seeing the problem. Obviously, I don't have issues with only buying clothing when it's "necessary".

- **Work Clothes** - We want to buy new clothes to raise our self-esteem, and many of us work in industries where people are well dressed and never wear the same outfit twice. If that describes your work environment, then modifying your clothing budget is going to be hard to do. Peer pressure doesn't end with high school or college. People that judge you based on the clothing you wear simply grow up, get jobs, and continue to do the same thing in the workplace.
- **School Clothes** – Clothing related peer pressure is definitely more difficult if you have children that go to school in an environment where an emphasis is placed on being dressed well.

    Prior to my real estate career, I was in the Loss Prevention Industry for five years. Without extensively thinking about it, I couldn't even put a number on the amount of teenagers that I detained for shoplifting over a five year period. I can tell you that 90% of them were stealing clothes to fit in with their peers.

As Americans we tend to define ourselves by our materialistic possessions. I can promise you that you are you, and your kids are your kids, regardless of what they wear, what you drive, and where you live. The hardest part of The Divorce Diet is to remember that and to keep a positive self-image while you are losing possessions that you feel define who you are.

Transportation & Gas

Unless you live in NYC or somewhere that has an excellent public transportation system, and you live in the US, then I'm guessing that you have a car payment, car insurance, and you have to pay for gas, oil changes, and other maintenance to your vehicle. For most Americans our car payments can be the equivalent to or exceed the amount that we pay for shelter. We love our cars don't we!

What are you currently paying per month for all of those items put together? As far as speaking of psychological attachments go, most of us are emotionally attached to our vehicles. Unfortunately, some of us feel that our vehicle also defines who we are. So, how much does your definition of yourself cost you?

When I was in real estate, I felt it was important to drive a nice vehicle. If I met you at a house for a viewing and my car was falling apart, what would you think? I'm guessing you would think that I'm not very good at my profession and that you should probably find someone who is successful in their industry. If you're a successful person then you drive an expensive reputable vehicle, right?? The car I pull up in has nothing to do with my intellectual expertise, however, many of us are defined in that manner just the same.

When I left my ex I had retired from real estate to write full time and finish my psychology degree. I "owned" (if you're making a car payment then you don't "own" your vehicle, you are leasing it from the finance company regardless of what the paperwork tells you) a BMW X3 and paid almost $900 monthly for the car payment and insurance alone. My last few years in real estate I had crossed over to the other side of the closing table and I was an Escrow Officer. My monthly bonus would typically exceed the $900 a month spent on my vehicle, so not having to use any part of my salary towards those expenses justified the costs and made economical sense to me at the time. What happened when I left my ex as a retiree and a full-time student? Well, I ended up driving a 1992 Honda Accord with 351,500 miles that's what. I should have mentioned earlier that with all of my new recipes I became very accustomed to eating "humble pie".

Your vehicle is most likely your biggest expense outside of what you pay for shelter. Whether or not you want to, you may be forced to downgrade, and additionally, some of you may lose your vehicle all together.

To most of us, losing your vehicle completely fits the "Devastation" category. Most Americans don't have a great mental image of using public transportation. You have to wait on it, you have to share it with people that you may not want to sit next to, you may have to take multiple buses, routes, etc. to get to your final destination which may cause you to have to leave for work hours earlier than you would've if you could drive yourself. Overall, it doesn't seem to be a pleasant experience. Some feel that it is a punishment, as opposed to a privilege.

Do you know what I think when I see people at bus stops? I immediately think, "There is a person with motivation!" How many times have you heard someone say, "I couldn't make it because I had car trouble", or "I couldn't make it because I didn't have a ride." Those aren't reasons, they're excuses used by people with no motivation to get where they need to go. Just because you can't get there in comfort, doesn't typically mean that you can't get there at all.

If you breakdown your budget and realize that you are going to have to choose between your vehicle or your shelter as opposed to simply downgrading, I'm guessing that if you don't have a friend or family member to live with, you're going to choose shelter over your vehicle. Although that can seem like a very shocking and devastating decision to make, think about the dollar amount that you will save each month.

Always try to avoid a "Repossession". Try trading your car for a car with less payments. If that doesn't work, then research companies that will buy your car from you without you having to purchase a new one. Look into finding someone to take over the Note/loan for you, which will require them to be approved for a completely new loan, but this is worked out through the current lender without having to work with a dealership. If none of those options work, ask if a "Voluntary Repossession", which is where you surrender your car to the finance company, will help with your situation at all.

> **Car payments & insurance** – As I stated above, if you make a car payment then car "ownership" is just a word used to get you to feel good about yourself while you pay a finance company and allow them to keep part of the payment, aka "interest". If you think I'm wrong and that you do "own" it, then great try not paying that car payment and let me know how long you get to keep what you "own". Owning a vehicle, means that you have the title to the vehicle in your possession and that there are no liens against it. Only then do you truly "own" a vehicle that can't be taken away from you.

   An average car payment for older vehicles is $300, and car insurance for full coverage is $150, so most Americans with car payments spend an average of $450 not including gas or maintenance fees.

> What amount do you spend each month? Now take that amount and multiply it by 6. That's what you will save over a six month

period if you decide to not have a car payment. Now multiply it by 12, and that is what you will save over a period of a year.
- The average cost of $450 x 12 months = $5,400.00 yearly. What could you do if you were able to save yourself over $5,000 a year? I'm guessing a lot! I think saving thousands of dollars is worth some extra time spent getting where you need to go, and the occasional unpleasant commuter at your side.
- **GAS!** - We haven't even touched on the price of gas or total cost of getting that vehicle of yours where it needs to take you. This will also depend on the area or region you live in. The price of gas is always going to fluctuate, as Americans we know this very well, so you never want to back yourself into a corner where you're paying for a vehicle that you can't afford to put gas in.

    Looking at your bank account, how much do you spend on gas each month? As far as "necessary spending" goes, this is the area where it will be very difficult to adjust cost. Even if you change the vehicle you're driving, this cost could still remain the same.

    If you are changing cars and your gas budget is limited, then you need to look for the most economical car possible so that you're getting the most miles out of the gas money that you're spending.

- **Discounted gas** – Luckily my favorite place to shop for groceries also offers $0.10 off the price of a gallon of gas for every $100 that you spend at the store. Well, finally I'm back up to spending about $150 a week on groceries so every time I go to fill up my gas tank, I get anywhere from $0.10 - $0.50 off depending on how many weeks have past since the last time I bought gas. If you have any program like this in your area, I highly recommend it!
- **Toll fees** - I started out my real estate career in Dallas, TX working for a builder. I bought my home next to the community I was selling out of, yet there was another community that was struggling that they wanted me to report to, and finish closing out. When I made that change, I had to drive 50 minutes one way, and use two different tollways to get there. I spent $450 a month just to get back and forth from work!   I know that this is extreme but some of you

are facing this same dilemma. If you live in a large city and live on one side, yet work on another, you are most likely spending serious time and serious money to get where you need to be. Your only options here are to carpool, use public transportation, or get another job, none of which are optimal or comfortable to deal with.

Shelter

Your "home", whether it be a house, condo, apartment, trailer, or RV is the most important place and space that you have. Since divorced partners don't typically live together after the divorce, at least one of you, if not both of you are about to have to make a change in this area whether you like it or not.

In the event that you have to move from your current residence, you MUST communicate with your mortgage company or with your rental management company to try to avoid being involved in a Foreclosure or in an Eviction. If you own your home you can try to sell it on a Short Sale, or you can also file Bankruptcy and "Surrender" your home in the terms of the bankruptcy. As a renter, if you will be breaking your lease because you can't afford to stay, you need to communicate with the management office to sign "Reletting Fee" papers. Every lease has a "Reletting Fee" in the event that you break your lease. Being charged this fee is much better than having an Eviction on your credit so it is important to communicate with them immediately so that you will have better control of the situation. Keep in mind that most property management companies will not rent to you if you owe a reletting fee to anyone so getting this paid in full has to be a top priority.

Once you have determined exactly how much money you have to spend on rent or a mortgage then you're ready to start looking. Based on your budget you may have to go from everyone having their own room, to siblings sharing rooms, etc. Again, this will add stress to the already stressful situation but its better than receiving an Eviction notice or a Foreclosure letter trying to hang on to something you can't afford.

Depending on the age of your children you may want to involve them in this process. Budgeting involves elementary level mathematics so any child over the age of 7 can most likely help you put your full amount of income on paper, then list out your debts and grocery or spending budget, then use a calculator to subtract them, which will leave the amount left for your shelter budget. We will cover this in the Personal Finance Workbook section so if you feel comfortable sharing that with you children, then you should.

If you involve your children in the new home search process, they may be more understanding of the situation and it may also help them feel a sense of control in a situation that they were unable to control, the splitting of their family. Most children are extremely intelligent and trying to hide things from them will only frustrate them further. While they may not need to know the details of the reason for the split, they should be involved in future decisions that directly involve them to allow them to regain some solid ground.

If you're moving to a new area, research the school in that area and drive by the school to let your children see the place they will be attending. Let them play on the playground on the weekend prior to moving so that they will feel more familiar and comfortable once the move is complete. For older children help them research the extracurricular activities at the school and try to attend a game prior to moving. If you have a child like me who would rather be by themselves with a great book, then simply research libraries or book stores in the area.

> **Subletting TO someone** – For those of you that own your home and are determined to keep it, yet will struggle to pay the mortgage, you may want to try subletting space to another person and charging them rent that will compensate for the second income you lost when your spouse moved out.

    Be sure to print out a Rental Agreement and in the Special Provisions write out what the money they are paying you monthly applies to. If they can only pay one set amount then be sure that the amount includes utilities, internet access, and any other expenses you have that they will be partaking in. Also, be sure to set predetermined times for showers, cooking meals in the kitchen, and how much space in the refrigerator is to go to them, as well as an area in the pantry or cabinets for their dry goods or kitchen equipment.

Be cautious who you let into your space and do research on Renter's Rights and Squatters Rights in your area. Just because someone is supposed to pay you rent, doesn't necessarily mean that they will. The chance of someone NOT paying you INCREASES if you let a friend or family member move in with you. Because you're their "friend" or a member of their "family" surely, you'll understand if they're going through a financial difficulty and can't pay you, right? WRONG!

It will be much harder emotionally to "evict" a friend or family member that isn't paying you as opposed to an acquaintance or a stranger that you vetted prior to letting them move in.

ALWAYS check the previous rental history and criminal history of anyone BEFORE you let them into your place and your space. Devious people typically have an excellent script and are able to portray themselves as very responsible and honorable. Most of us get divorced because our ex-spouse had a great script! Remember that actions speak louder than words and to apply that in all dealings with other human beings under any circumstances.

I did not state to check their credit score simply because as we'll discuss further, someone's credit can be ruined by another person or through life circumstances. My credit score went from a 750+ down to a 480, yet I NEVER paid my rent late. The fact that I paid my rent on time and in full did not help my credit score because it wasn't reflected through the bureaus, however the fact that I was unable to pay my credit cards because I needed to pay my rent, completely ruined my credit during that time period.

➢ **Renting a house** – If you will be renting a new house, be sure to ask the home owner or landlord what the utilities will run so that you are sure that you can afford all of the bills. Older homes or homes with older windows will typically have higher utilities due to insulation issues. If you're moving from a new construction home that has newer technology for insulation and heating/cooling units then you may be shocked by the utilities in a smaller square foot home made decades previously. They could be the same, or they could even be higher.

Be sure to pay attention to any yard maintenance you will be required to do. If your ex-spouse kept all of the yard equipment because they did the yard work, will you have to buy a new lawn mower, trimmer, pruners, etc.? Make sure that you are prepared for all expenses in advance.

Always disclose all pets that you have. Thinking that the home owner won't notice your dog or cat could cause serious issues later, and you don't want to be in violation of your lease agreement due to your pet, which for most of us, is one of our favorite family members.

> **Renting an apartment or condo** – When looking for an apartment be sure to ask about the different lease terms. For some of you, the circumstance may be that you will be selling the home that you owned with your ex-spouse which will give you seller's proceeds after the closing to use to buy another home, or will allow you to afford a larger place by putting it in savings and using it for future budgeting. In these cases, try looking for a month-to-month or six month lease term so that you will not have to pay reletting fees if you sign a year lease and are ready to move before the year is completed.

If you know that your financial situation will most likely be set for an extended period of time, look for places that have one or more year lease terms. These will typically be lower in rent and you will be able to focus on other parts of your life without having to worry about moving expenses coming back into budget within the year.

Once again, always disclose all pets that you have. Thinking the management company won't notice your dog or cat could be a lease violation that you do not want to have to deal with.

Do you have a large dog that is typically against lease agreement policies? If you happen to live in a state like Colorado, then if a dog has been permitted as an Emotional Support Animal then the breed is typically irrelevant to the lease terms. Look into these types of programs and rights in your area.

> **Subletting FROM someone** – If you find yourself in the unfortunate category of DEVASTATION where you are unable to retain your residence on your own, or to even find anything that you can afford by yourself, one option is to sublet a room or rooms from someone else.

Again, it is important to research Renter's rights and Squatter's rights in your area before you go into an agreement with anyone. Unfortunately, I found myself in this situation and two weeks after paying for a room the home owner made it clear that she didn't want us there anymore. Well, I did not have the money to move and we had agreed upon a six month term so now what? Our subletting situation went from bad to worse so be very cautious who you trust to sublet from. There is no shortage of people that will want to take your money, then also want you to leave once they've received it.

One of my favorite things that Oprah says is, "Believe who people are the first time they tell you." Meaning, if a person has an established pattern of behavior, don't let them try to convince you that they are anything but the way they are known for acting or behaving. If people are known for being chaotic and having volatile relationships with people they have lived with, don't think that you will be an exception to that just because you've never had issues with them previously. People are who they are and aren't going to change because you're going through a difficult time.

In most Caucasian cultures there is no such thing as family caring for family so in my personal experience and in some of my client's real estate experiences, I have multiple examples of families that get tired of someone, so they tell them to "get out" with no regard for where they go or what happens to them. I highly caution you against moving in with friends or family unless you are very close to them and you are positive that this won't happen. Since you're going through a divorce then you are very familiar with the fact that you can't control or trust people that you love and consider to be family in all circumstances, so proceed with caution!

Before moving in be sure to talk about whether or not the agreed upon amount includes utilities, internet access, and the rotation or schedule of showers, kitchen usage, and space in the refrigerator and pantry/cabinets. Although you may not think these are major issues, I know from personal experience that they absolutely can be if you sublet from the wrong person.

Get everything in writing!! If you know the person you will be subletting from, then they will most likely want you to give them the money and agree to terms with a smile and a handshake, however this can come into play later and it will be their word against yours, which will make you a "Squatter" instead of a "Renter".

- **Shelters** – Most of us do not even want to think about having to live in a shelter. I myself was too prideful to research shelters or temporary housing and deciding to sublet a room for us was a serious mistake on my part. I wish I would have instead chosen to look at family shelter situations where we would have had our own room and a safe environment.

   Staying in a shelter where there are no individual rooms, but simply multi use cots in a large area where people filter in and out daily is definitely not something that most of us would want to do whether or not we have children. This option would be the least optimal, however you would be provided with a warm place to sleep and a hot meal as opposed to living in your car, or other scenarios that could be dangerous and even more devastating.

   Before making any final decisions be sure to reach out to community programs and surrounding churches that have programs for income based housing or temporary housing, prior to making any final decisions.

   The place you live and sleep is the most important decision that will be made during this process.

Credit Cards

While some could argue that credit cards aren't a "necessary" expense, it is absolutely "necessary" to continue to pay them if you want to keep your credit score in good standing.

In the realm of the categories we've listed for "necessary" spending, this is the area that you have the most area of fluctuation with. Some creditors will allow you to put your card into a status that holds spending but allows you to make small payments that will keep the account in good standing until you are able to financially recover and put the account back into a regular status.

For some of you, this also will be an area where complete loss may occur. In my case, I had seven credit cards when I left my ex. I called each of them and explained the situation, to which they responded, "I'm sorry to hear that, no you can't make any less than your minimum payment, and when will you be making that payment?" Like I said previously, when I only had $20 for food for two weeks, and it was imperative to pay my rent in full and on time, I had no choice but to watch my credit score plummet into the depths of darkness because I was unable to keep up with the payments. We will discuss how to recover from this situation in the "Building or Re-Building Credit" and "Collections" sections.

Savings

One of the most important things that you can do with your money is to take it out of your checking account, and put it into your savings account, aka Paying Yourself! "Life" is always going to happen, therefore the more money you have in savings, the better prepared you'll be to handle it.

Once you've set a fixed budget most people tend to spend the money outside of what is needed for expenses on extra things like shopping and entertainment. That's all great while everything is going smoothly but what happens if you suddenly need a new tire, or repairs to your car that you hadn't planned on and those repairs are not covered by a warranty of any kind? If you don't have any money in savings to deal with it then you may get very familiar with the section on not having a vehicle, simply because you're unable to afford the repairs.

"Borrowing" money from others should be a last resort. If you are on a fixed budget and already don't have the money for the issue, how will you be able to pay that "borrowed" money back? You would more likely be asking someone to "give" you money because you won't have the means to pay them back. As most people know this can cause issues with the person that you "borrowed" the money from, simply because they are expecting you to pay them back at some point. If this is absolutely necessary, you need to be up front about the fact that you may not be able to pay them back.

I can promise you that cutting out that extra spending to "pay yourself" by putting money in savings will make you feel much better than asking someone else for help. While you are creating your monthly budget determine how much you are able to transfer to savings and be sure and stick to it.

Most major issues will cost anywhere from $500 - $2,000 so if you have any less than that in your savings account, you aren't prepared for a major issue, and therefore you should only take money out of the account if it is a necessity. Most Americans have less than $500 in savings, and the majority of Americans do not have any money in savings at all.

Let's say that you have $50 in savings but suddenly it's time for school pictures which will cost $20. Do you take the $20 out of savings to pay for school pictures? I would say yes because most kids are getting packs of pictures, but it would depend on what you and your child want. Now, let's say that you only have $50 in savings and your child wants to go to the mall with their friends and spend $20. Do you pull that out of savings, or do you say that you don't have it? My kids all know that I would say "I'm sorry, I don't have any money", but some of you may feel that it is important to let your child do this if it is a special occasion.

The point is that once you put money in savings, it should be viewed as "not having it". If you have $200 in savings and $30 in your checking account and your kids ask you how much money you have, the answer is $30. Your savings is there for emergencies only or to put aside for a greater goal later down the road, not set aside for entertainment. You are already supposed to be budgeting for entertainment so if you need to pull money out of savings to be entertained, then in actuality you don't have the money for entertainment in your budget.

Even if you can only put $10 per week aside or $20 bi-weekly with your paycheck, that will be $40 a month, $240 every six months, and $480 by the end of the year. If you celebrate Christmas and you're already worried about what you're going to do for Christmas gifts, try this and if you start at the beginning of the year then by Christmas, you'll have almost $500 to spend.

Some of you may be thinking that $500 is a low amount for Christmas, however there are plenty of people who can't afford to celebrate Christmas and would love to have $500 for a nice meal and presents.

When my second son was born, he had several health issues and we had a restricted budget. That year our 9-year-old stated that he wanted a Playstation for Christmas. I told him that I wasn't sure if I could afford it, but that I would try. To this he responded, "It's okay I already told Santa Claus that's what I wanted so he'll get it for me!" WHAT!?! I will say that I had already purchased the Playstation but I wasn't about to let "Santa Claus" get all the glory because I had saved up money to buy it for him.

I contemplated telling my son that Santa is no longer around and that it's the parents responsibility to keep the tradition going because he was at an age where this was about to become evident regardless, however I responded with this statement, "Santa Claus has to buy toys for every child on earth so I can promise you that he doesn't spend more than $20 per child. If you get a Playstation it will be because I bought it for you." My son thought about that for a minute, then said, "Okay that makes sense", and walked off. Whew!

Holidays and birthdays are the hardest things to deal with when you are going through financial difficulties. I believe it is important to inform your children of the actual reason for the holiday, which typically isn't about spending money.

One good practice would be to tell your children the amount that you have to spend and ask them to write out 5 – 10 things that are within that budget. Set the understanding that they will only get a few of the items on the list which will total the amount allotted for all of their gifts combined. If they want something expensive then they will have to realize that they may only get one item. Try to be creative when it comes to holiday budgeting so that everyone can still maintain a positive attitude and enjoy each other, which is the point of spending holidays together.

Does your banking institution have any programs that help with holidays? When I lived in Amarillo, I was a member of a Credit Union and I had my car financed through them. In August and December both you had the option to "skip" a car payment so that you could use that money for vacations, school clothes or for holiday spending. While the interest still accrued, the payments were not "late" and were added to the end of your term. Search for banks and credit unions in your area to see if changing your banking institution can help you with additional savings.

Student Loans

If you are currently paying on student loans and you know it will be a struggle to continue to make these payments, call the creditor immediately to see if you qualify for a forbearance or any other program that will help you put your payments on hold.

If you haven't finished your degree or you wanted to further your education, then now is the time to look into your options for returning to school. If you are a full-time student, then you are not required to pay on your student loans in most cases. Obviously, you may have to take out additional loans to achieve this, but if you will be able to increase your salary when you complete your degree or get your secondary degree then I would recommend looking into this option.

Student loans are one of the easiest things to keep under control because multiple companies will help you refinance or restructure your loans. These are also one of the most detrimental loans to be delinquent on because student loans being in "default" will significantly decrease your scores. Even if all other areas of your credit are in good standing, by these loans being in default your credit score will most likely remain low until these are under control.

Now that we've taken a hard look at your "Spending Habits" you now know exactly where you can modify your spending to be able to allocate that extra money to other areas of your budget. Once you've completed the full analysis of your spending habits you are ready to use the Personal Finance Workbook section to help you determine exactly what category you fall into:

- UNCOMFORTABLE = Modification of spending habits to adjust to one income.
- STRUGGLE = The need to downsize your home, vehicle, or both in addition to modifying your spending habits.

➢ DEVASTATION = Complete loss of home, vehicle, or both in addition to serious modification of your spending habits.

Regardless of which category you fall into, once you know where you stand you can set your budget, then begin to set personal goals to help you get back to a level where you will be happy and feel fulfilled.

Personal Finance Workbook

Current Monthly Expenses

*U*se this section to list all of your current monthly expenses. For utilities, groceries, gas, credit card payments, and other expenses that fluctuate, review your bank statements for the last 90 days to get an average of these expenses and place the average in the blank for those items.

- Mortgage/Rent = $_____
- Home Security = $_____
- Utilities - Electric and/or Gas = $_____
- Water and/or Trash service = $_____
- Home phone = $_____
- Cell phone = $_____
- Internet = $_____
- Cable or TV services = $_____
- Car payment = $_____
- Car insurance = $_____
- Car maintenance = $_____
- Groceries = $_____
- Work lunches = $_____
- School lunches = $_____
- Eating out = $_____
- Credit card payments = $_____

- Shopping for clothes/tangible items = $_____
- Entertainment = $_____
- _____ = $_____
- _____ = $_____
- **Total of all average Monthly Expenses = $_____**

Current Monthly Breakdown

$_____ = Current Monthly Net Income
- $_____ = Current Monthly Expenses
= $_____ = Total amount left after expenses

How much do you have left after subtracting your current monthly expenses from the total of your monthly net income?

If this amount is positive, then determine if the total amount is enough to begin putting money into savings or reserves. If this amount is not enough to last you comfortably until your next paycheck and/or to put money aside then return to the Spending Habits section to look for areas to save money by reducing your spending.

If this amount is negative, then you are in the RED and you will need to modify your monthly expenses. Return to the Spending Habits section to analyze your spending to determine if you can adjust your budget by changing some of the ways you spend your monthly income.

Modified Monthly Expenses

After reviewing the Spending Habits section determine what areas of your monthly expenses can be modified by changing the way you spend money on a monthly basis. Enter the new amounts below.

- Mortgage/Rent = $_____
- Home Security = $_____
- Utilities - Electric and/or Gas = $_____
- Water and/or Trash service = $_____
- Home phone = $_____
- Cell phone = $_____
- Internet = $_____

- Cable or TV services = $_____
- Car payment = $_____
- Car insurance = $_____
- Car maintenance = $_____
- Groceries = $_____
- Work lunches = $_____
- School lunches = $_____
- Eating out = $_____
- Credit card payments = $_____
- Shopping for clothes/tangible items = $_____
- Entertainment = $_____
- _____ = $_____
- _____ = $_____
- **Total of all modified Monthly Expenses = $_____**

Modified Monthly Breakdown

$_____ = Current Monthly Net Income
- $_____ = Modified Monthly Expenses
= $_____ = Total amount left after expenses

How much do you have left after subtracting your modified monthly expenses from the total of your monthly net income?

If this amount is positive, then determine if the total amount is enough to begin putting money into savings or reserves. If this amount is not enough to last you comfortably until your next paycheck and to put money aside, or if you have a negative amount, then you will need to determine if you are able to make changes to your mortgage/rent and/or car payments.

Review the Shelter and Car Expenses section for ideas to save money by making changes in these two areas. After you have determined your options for modifying or downsizing your Shelter and Car Expenses, input the last of your budget modifications below to set your final budget.

- Mortgage/Rent = $_____
- Home Security = $_____
- Utilities - Electric and/or Gas = $_____
- Water and/or Trash service = $_____

- Home phone = $_____
- Cell phone = $_____
- Internet = $_____
- Cable or TV services = $_____
- Car payment = $_____
- Car insurance = $_____
- Car maintenance = $_____
- Groceries = $_____
- Work lunches = $_____
- School lunches = $_____
- Eating out = $_____
- Credit card payments = $_____
- Shopping for clothes/tangible items = $_____
- Entertainment = $_____
- _____ = $_____
- _____ = $_____
- **Total of all final modified Monthly Expenses = $_____**

How much do you have left after subtracting your final modified monthly expenses from the total of your monthly net income?

If this amount is positive, then determine if the total amount is enough to begin putting money into savings or reserves. If this amount is not enough to last you comfortably until your next paycheck and to put money aside, or if you have a negative amount, then you will need to determine your areas of loss.

Review the Personal Goals section to determine areas that will help you to create MSI's or Multiple Sources of Income, however until you are able to generate that extra income you must determine what areas on your expenses list will be dropped from the monthly budget.

Once you have the final budget set you will then need to determine which expenses will be paid with your rotation of paychecks. Use a calendar or phone app to write down exactly what bills/expenses you will be paying on your payday, and do not deviate from this plan.

In the next Setting Your Budget section, we will further discuss that you should always have your bills predetermined on your budget and mapped out on your calendar for 90 days in advance. Don't pay bills in a sporadic manner by hoping you'll have the money on the day they are due, or later than they are due. Pay every bill you have on one of your paydays only, and prior to when the bill is due. In addition, ALWAYS pay your bills on your payday PRIOR to leaving for the day to determine the exact amount you will have to utilize until your next payday arrives.

Finally, review your bank account daily and never go by your "Available Balance", the bills you pay will be drafted on different days, therefore you MUST know exactly how much is left after your expenses are paid in full and you must monitor your bank account daily to verify when each expense is posted to your account. When each payment posts notate "Paid" on your calendar or app until all items have been posted/drafted from your account.

Take the time now to finalize your budget, determine the day you will be paying each expense, and then place the expenses on the pre-determined dates for the next 90 day period. After a month passes, add the next month to your budget plan so that you always have a 90 day "map" of your expenses and the day they will be paid.

Setting Your Budget

At this point you should have used the Workbook to determine your monthly budget. You should know exactly how much money you have for all of your "Necessary" spending, and you should have determined whether or not you have money left over for "Unnecessary" spending.

The best practices for staying on budget are the following:

- Budget everything! Think of every possible scenario and write it down to be certain that you are covering all needed expenses. Remember to budget for your savings account so that you will have the money set aside for any unforeseen issues that may arise.
- Use a calendar, planner, or an app on your phone to put all of your bills on your paydays so that you know exactly what will be paid and when. Do this for 3 months in advance so that for the next 90 days you will see exactly where your money is going. Always keep 90 days worth of bills on the calendar.
- Waiting until the "bill is due" could cause you to spend the money for the bill in advance, therefore you need to pay bills on your specific paydays and in advance of when they are due.
- In most cases your rent or mortgage and utilities are due at the beginning of the month so you would pay these with your first check of the month, or your last check of the month depending on how the dates fall into play.

- Try to make your car payment and other expenses to be due around the middle of the month so that you can handle those bills with your mid-month paycheck.
- <u>On payday, pay your bills BEFORE you leave the house!</u> Most of us these days have our pay checks direct deposited and we either pay our bills online or over the phone. Even if you still write checks you can write them before you leave the house.
  - Bills typically don't get paid because we get our paychecks then start spending, then only after we've spent money on what we want, do we then address what needs to be paid. By paying your bills before you even leave the house you can be certain that all of your bills will be paid on time and in full!
  - Check your balance daily!! Every morning before you leave the house check your balance to be certain that the bills you have paid have been taken out of your account. Never check your balance by simply looking at the "Available Balance". Certain creditors will take up to 3 business days to take the funds out of your account. ALWAYS verify that the items have been removed and that the "Available Balance" matches the amount that you previously determined would be left after paying bills.
  - Every payday you should know EXACTLY how much money you have left to last you until the next payday. You will begin each payday by writing down your balance, subtracting each bill you will pay, then using the amount left over to determine money that can be spent on groceries, gas, and other necessities, then circle the remaining amount and verify that this is correct on a daily basis until the next payday.
  - Too many people will say, "I didn't expect that to come out of my account", or "I didn't know that was going to come out of my account", which is something that no one should ever say! It is your money, and it is your bank account. Ask yourself right now how much is in your account/s and if the answer is "I don't know", then that is the wrong answer!
  - Right now, I have Amazon Prime, Netflix, Hulu, Spotify, DropBox, and a Car Wash bill that all come out of my account on different dates, predetermined by those companies. For

those bills I simply note what dates that they will be drafted from my account and I put those amounts on the bills due on the payday that I allotted to pay them, which is always the payday before they are drafted.

- Again, just because your "Available Balance" says you have $100 available, you may not. For example, if the six things I listed above will be taken out before my next paycheck then I actually only have $30, not $100.
- Don't let anything "surprise" you. Life is difficult to control so enjoy the fact that once you budget your money and expenses, that could literally be the ONLY area of your life that you have control of. Trying to control people is futile at times, controlling your money is EASY once you set yourself up for success by staying on top of everything.
- Never use overdraft protection! If you have it, get rid of it immediately! If your first response is to say, "But I use it every month, I can't get rid of it", then I want you to go into your bank account and add up all of the fees that you paid the bank for using this feature in the last month.

I'm guessing the charges are at least $30 per transaction and that you have multiple transactions which could range anywhere from $60 - $240+. Now think about what you could have bought with that money, or the fact that you could have put that money into savings instead of giving it to the bank. Let me rephrase that, you didn't give it to them, they took it from you for allowing you to use money in advance of when you actually had it to spend.

If you budget your money as suggested, you will never need to use this feature again. Banking institutions make a lot of money from overdraft fees so don't be surprised if they try to talk you out of turning this feature off. Smile at them and let them know that you've got it under control and that you no longer need it.

How Your Credit Affects Your Lifestyle

Okay! So, you've made all of your budget and spending changes and now you're feeling great about yourself! That is until you check your mail or your phone rings. For those of you that had no choice but to let credit card payments go, or that went through major issues involving your credit, you are most likely experiencing the fallout from those creditors coming at you for the money you owe them.

When you set your personal goals, one of the main goals should be to "get out of debt". Getting out of debt means different things to different people. Some of you will have to first obtain personal goals of creating MSI's or Multiple Sources of Income or obtaining that degree for a better paycheck before you can even begin to get into credit repair. If that's the case, then that is typical for most people, the key is to get started as soon as possible, and to take on one thing at a time.

➢ Credit Scores

What is a credit score anyway? In almost ten years of real estate I had that question asked many times. Since the majority of Americans get what they need on "credit" our entire world of spending seems to revolve around that concept. Saving up the money to pay for something in full seems ridiculous when you can simply get what you want when you want on "credit".

People unfamiliar with credit scores tend to think that if you're a "good person" then of course you will have a good credit score. It has more to do with your character than it does with anything else right? Wrong!

The word "score" should make you think of a "game". That's exactly what your credit score is based off of, how well you play the "game of credit". If you never purchase anything on credit and you pay cash for everything, you could have hundreds of thousands of dollars in the bank, yet you will have a very low credit score. Whereas if you only have $10 in the bank, but you pay everything you have purchased on credit on time and in the amount agreed upon, then your score is most likely very high.

Your credit score is based off of how well you repay money that was advanced to you as "credit". You're advanced or given a certain amount of money which the creditor gave you based on the fact that you would repay that money within a certain amount of time, and at a set time and amount each month. The way in which you comply with the terms of the credit advancement directly affects your score.

What about credit cards? You were given a set credit "limit" and given a minimum payment, so if you max out that card, then as long as you pay your minimal payments your score will be good right? Wrong! In reference to credit cards if that balance is maxed out then your score will decrease until the balance is under around 20% of the total credit line that you have on that card. So, for a credit card with a $500 limit, if you have a balance of more than $100 it could begin to negatively affect your score.

What if you have credit cards with high lines of credit but never use them at all, then your score will look fantastic right? Wrong again! As I said before this is a "game", so you have to actually use the credit for your score to be reflected. Inactivity on accounts could affect your score in a negative manner instead of a positive one, depending on the time it has been dormant and the length of time that the account has been open.

For optimal credit scores you should pay all loan payments on time and in full (always add additional money towards the principal when possible), and for all credit cards you should keep a balance between 10% and 20% of the total credit line and pay it off in full each month when the bill is due.

Luckily, we currently have multiple credit monitoring platforms that will show you what your credit score is and will also reflect what accounts are in good standing, as well as those that are "in the red" or being negatively reflected on your credit reports. The platforms that are free will typically show you a higher score than those that are used by lenders, mortgage companies, and other financial institutions that pull your credit. The reason is that there are different scoring programs and your score will be based on the program being used by the creditor you are attempting to get a line of credit through.

While the fact that the exact score may vary, what does not vary, is who you owe money to and how much money you owe. Not all creditors report to all three credit bureaus. Some report to all three, some report to two, and some to only one. The three main bureaus are Equifax, Experian, and TransUnion. Most free platforms will only show you two of the three, but at least that is a start. You can pay a minimal monthly expense to be able to see all three bureaus scores and reported debt through a variety of companies, so if you feel you need to see all three, then research into those.

The best part about the free apps is that there is typically a direct link to the creditors that you owe money to. You can click on the debt being showed and it will most likely give you the creditors address and phone number. On my favorite app you simply click the phone number to the creditor, and you will instantly be calling them.

Open accounts that are not being paid on time will absolutely drop your score. Closed accounts that are in "collections" will also drop your score and keep it low until they are taken care of and shown to have a $0 balance due.

➢ How do credit scores impact your life?

Well, unless you have cash to pay for where you live, what you drive, and any other major purchase that you may need, then your credit score directly affects your life.

In Colorado your rental history is pretty much irrelevant to most property management companies. Unless you have a 600 Fico score and for some companies a 650, it doesn't matter what your previous rental history looks like.

To have the ability to purchase a home, most mortgage companies want to see a credit score of over 640, but some will tell you that you can have as low as a 580 with 20% down, which most people don't have. For a home priced at $100,000 (which is quite low in most areas), you would need $20,000 down to qualify for that loan. I'm assuming that if you had $20,000 then your score wouldn't be that low in the first place, but there are always exceptions to every scenario.

When buying a home, the lower your credit score is, the higher the interest rate is. Use a mortgage calculator (search for one online) and play around with different interest rates so that you can see how much the house payment is directly affected by the interest rate that you are given. A higher rate could mean a mortgage payment that is $200 - $300 per month higher than your neighbor living in a comparable house, yet with a better credit score and interest rate.

When you go to purchase a car your interest rate is also determined by your credit score. What that means is that if your interest rate is high, then every time you make a payment, the majority of the payment is kept by the creditor and only a minimal amount will go towards your principal.

This means that every time you make that monthly car payment, the total amount you owe barely fluctuates. They are literally pocketing money and banking off of your low credit score. That's exactly why so many car companies will say, "No Credit No Problem!", they are going to make a serious amount of money simply because you don't have your finances under control.

➢ How long does it take to repair your credit?

That was my favorite question for a client to ask me! Most people live a lifestyle of dealing with bad credit. Having good credit seems impossible to most people therefore, why bother!

The majority of people don't get serious about wanting to repair their credit until they truly want to purchase a home. It is more evident at that point in time to have your finances and credit score under control simply because you will not see a mortgage lender with a banner that says, "No Credit, No Problem!"

Having bad credit is a huge problem when it comes to purchasing a home because a human being can trash a house, aka the asset, before the mortgage company can "foreclose" or get it back from them. The potential for loss to the mortgage company is extremely high, therefore they are more cautious with who they loan money to, and under what terms.

Car companies are more willing to lend to people with bad credit because they can simply pull up to your car while you're not in it and take it! Done and done!

My answer to anyone that asked me how long it will take to repair their credit was, "Let me look at your credit report and let's talk about your budget, and I will be able to give you an exact timeframe."

As I stated previously, I had clients for many years, so I have a ton of examples to share with you, but I am going to use one of my favorite client's stories, and my own story to give you two examples.

> **1st example** – I was working as a Sales Manager for a builder and I had a woman come to me with her credit report in hand and she was looking for Seller Financing because she had applied for a mortgage loan but had been turned down due to the fact that she had a score of 525. The loan officer that had pulled her credit knew me and knew the company I worked for so he told her to come and see me because I would be able to help her get into a home.
>
> I looked at her credit report and she didn't have any derogatory credit on her report, she simply hadn't used any credit at all in the last five years. Five years previously she had gone through a divorce, so all of her credit card accounts were closed, and she was driving a van that was paid in full. Therefore, the only things she spent money on; rent, car insurance, utilities, and groceries, were never reflected on her credit report. She had "bad credit" simply because she wasn't "playing the credit game".
>
> This woman made over $75,000 a year and was the single mother of four children. I told her that I could absolutely help her with Seller Financing, but that the interest rate would be 12%, however I believed that if she followed the instructions I was about to give her to boost her credit score, then by the time we were finished building her house, she could most likely get a 6% interest rate. When I showed her the difference in what her house payment would be at 12% vs. 6% she was absolutely on board to follow the plan I was going to give her!
>
> One other thing I want to add about this woman is her response when I told her the amount of home she qualified for. When you

work with a builder you have several different floorplans or prices to choose from. I showed her the best plan we had for a four bedroom home, which was also the most expensive. Based on her income and her debt, which obviously wasn't anything, I knew she could afford the most expensive home that we had to offer. She declined that floorplan and went with the least expensive four bedroom that we offered and said this to me, "I know I make a lot of money, but I have four kids, three that are teenage boys, and they won't stop eating or growing, so I need that money for food and clothes."

Well, Amen for having clients that are smart when it comes to how they spend money! Most people want the best of the best and they'll figure out how to pay for it later. For those of you that know what you need to spend on those areas, (which you should by now because we just finished using the Workbook to figure it out!) life will be much easier for you financially.

When you deal with new construction you pick your lot and your floorplan and the home is built from the ground up, so depending on the builder it can take up to six months to complete. This particular builder had a timeframe of four to five months, so it was imperative that she start following my instructions immediately. We wrote the contract for a four bedroom home at 12% interest for seller financing and once the contract was signed by the builder, the clock started ticking.

Instructions for Steps to Success = Obtain three lines of credit. Most mortgage companies want to see at least three lines of credit open, active, and in good standing. Some do business based on score only, however the lenders I was dealing with at that time, preferred to see a minimum of three different accounts.

When I told her this, her first response to me was, "But I don't have the money for credit cards!" Interesting statement! The majority of people think that a credit card is "fun money" or "extra" money to go out and make frivolous purchases with, or to finance their entertainment. Not true!

My response = "You spend money every day. The key is to put your debit card in the back of your wallet and use the credit card until you've reached 20% of the credit line, then switch back to using your debit card. When the bill comes each month, pay it off in full, then begin the rotation of using a credit card for gas and food until you've reached 20% again, and repeat this scenario for two different cards. You're spending the same amount of money the only change is the card you're using at the register."

Not only is this the best practice to keep your credit score high, and monthly spending low, in the event that your card is stolen it doesn't directly affect your bank account. Using a credit card for gas and groceries is much smarter and safer than using your debit card.

For the third credit line I sent her to a bank that I worked with that gives a credit line of $1,000 as a personal installment loan. For anyone with a credit score of under 600 this particular bank would put that money in a "savings account" which was under their control and would "release" the full amount after the loan had been paid in full. I'm not sure how many places do this because this was a scenario that I was able to create with the bank manager. That bank was local, and it was sitting right next to the subdivision that I was selling homes from and was two doors down from our main offices. The bank manager knew that his chances of getting more business increased if the home owners in the subdivision were using his bank, therefore he was on board to create the program, and it worked out great for many of my clients!

After one month her credit report reflected that she had two credit cards, and one installment loan of $1,000.00. After five months of paying on those credit cards as we had discussed, and paying that installment loan on time, her credit score had raised from a 525 to a 620!

She was able to obtain a traditional loan at 5.75% interest and we closed on her house with her having a house payment that was approximately $400 less than the initial quote, and with the builder happy that he received payment in full instead of having to carry the Note for her. It was an absolute WIN/WIN for everyone!

So, in this particular scenario, she went from pretty much no credit, to raising her credit score almost 100 points within a period of five months.

➤ **2nd example** – My Divorce Diet aftermath left me with a credit score of 480 which is extremely low! I had about thirty collections on my credit report which all pertained to only seven different credit cards, one reletting fee, an old utility bill, and an old cable bill.

When I left my ex all of those accounts began to start posting bad remarks on my credit report due to non-payment, and the accounts were eventually closed and sent to "collections."

I left my ex in May of 2015 and I was not in a position to begin addressing my credit issues until January of 2017, which was about a year and a half later. Over that period, my collections had been "sold" to multiple creditors. When one creditor sells your account to another, they typically don't care that it still shows as active on your report, so it will stay there until you dispute it. Therefore, out of the twenty-seven "collections" that were showing on my report, only ten of them were accurate.

- Step 1 = I signed up with a credit repair company that is also a law firm that will dispute charges on your behalf. I have used them before and I have referred several of my clients to them, and for my personal situation they always do a great job. They were able to take the twenty-seven collections showing down to the ten that were accurate, and then I was able to take it from there. They charge on a month to month basis, so I was able to cancel the service with no problems.
- Step 2 = Pay each collection, one at a time, until they show a $0.00 balance due. I was actually able to settle for about 60% - 70% of the full amounts, which I will discuss later in the "Collections" section.
- Step 3 = Establish "New Credit". Even if you pay off all of your old collections and accounts, your score will still only hang out at the bottom of the scoring range. As stated previously, you have to "play the credit game" if you want to have a good credit score.

Even though I was fine with the car that I had paid for in full, I knew I could get a car financed easier than I could get a credit card or loan, due to the fact that my score at this point was only about a 525.

I had determined that I could budget a car payment of no higher than $250, so I sold my car that was paid off to put a down payment on a car that was $6,500.00. I was tagged with a 21% interest rate due to my credit score at the time. I almost threw up all over the desk of the Finance Manager, but I knew I had to "play to win", so I signed on the dotted line knowing that I would be able to refinance the car in a year once my credit score had risen.

Additionally as a second form of credit I went to a furniture store that reports to the credit bureaus (don't make the mistake of getting furniture from a place that doesn't report to the bureaus because you're paying them an insane amount and not helping your credit at all) and got a new couch, TV, and a washer and dryer on "credit".

- Step 4 = The "waiting game" started. I obtained the two lines of credit above by April of 2017 and had paid off 4 of the 10 collections on my credit report. I knew I needed to have a score of around a 600 before trying to get any type of credit card, so I paid my car and furniture payments on time and continued to save money to pay off at least one collection each month.
- Step 5 = Pair up with a Mortgage Lender to determine what is needed to purchase a home. I began looking at houses through online apps and started getting contacted by an insane amount of Realtors that could see my activity. Obviously, I'm very biased in this area and I know exactly what type of Realtor I wanted to work with. I can tell you that people from Colorado aren't typically fans of people from Texas simply because Texans are known to be difficult to deal with. 100% true! We typically know exactly what we want and trying to get us to think differently is a waste of time. After avoiding about ten different Realtors I was finally contacted by someone I felt did business the way I did business. He listened to exactly what I wanted, and when I told him it would be about a year before I purchased he didn't blow me off, or try to talk me into applying for a loan I knew I wouldn't qualify for, instead he gave me the number of

a lender that he worked with and I was able to start the process of setting the goal to purchase a new home.

- Step 6 = By March of 2018 I knew my score was a 600 so I applied for a credit card and was approved for a $250 balance. I used the card in the manner in which I specified with my client (never exceed 20% and pay in full each month) and within three months they increased the credit limit to $500.

- Step 7 = Pay off all remaining debts and prepare to save the money needed to purchase a new home. I started talking to the Realtor and Lender about December of 2017. It took me until September of 2018 to have all of my debts paid, and to have built my credit score up to a 662. The lender had informed me that Colorado had a Down Payment Assistance Program which paid 100% of your required down payment if your credit score was above a 640. All I needed was the earnest money of $2,000 and the $700 needed for the appraisal, and we were ready to put a contract on a home. While I had been spending all of my extra money on paying off my old debts, my mother had acquired the $3,000.00 that I needed for the earnest money and appraisal, so she decided to give this money to me to help me quicken the home buying process. She was required to give the lender a "Gift Letter" in regards to the funds that were used.

- Step 8 = Home Buying Success! My realtor showed us only one home, which is the home I purchased. We researched multiple homes online and drove past them to get a feel for the neighborhoods, researched schools, and did all of the preliminary work, until we found the house that we had been looking for. We made an appointment for a showing, wrote the contract for the one and only house that he took us to look at, and a month later on October 31, 2018 I was able to purchase the home for $273,000 in my name only, all because I was able to create MSI's (Multiple Sources of Income) and repair my credit within a period of approximately 3.5 years.

- Reasons for Success = I put myself on a serious Divorce Diet over that 3.5 year period. How many clothes did I buy during that time? For myself, less than $100, for my son, as needed.

Since we LOVE food, I did budget in money to eat out once a weekend after I had put my MSI's in place.

How much money did I spend on entertainment and having "fun"? I spent $40 once a year for Jurassic Quest and Jurassic Tour because my son loves dinosaurs. I also bought a Family Pass to The Dinosaur Resource Center so that I could take my son to see that amazing place on the weekends with no additional charge. Aside from those things, we had fun for "free" and the little bits of money that I did spend for art supplies were minimal and all in my budget plan. I spent $0.00 outside of my budget.

So, back to the original question of "How long does it take to repair your credit?" The answer depends on your personal financial situation and your current credit report. It could take months, or it could take years. Either way, it depends on your dedication to committing to getting out of debt so that you can live an abundant lifestyle, instead of always looking for signs that say, "No Credit No Problem!".

Once you have reached the level that you can be approved for whatever you want, whenever you want it, you won't want to settle for anything less. Everyone falls, the difference between people is who gets up and makes plans to climb higher, and who lays there feeling that all they will ever achieve is failure. Again, you get out of life what you put into it. If you think that you're going to create a great lifestyle for yourself by doing nothing but complaining about your life, then you're wrong. You will always struggle. If you commit to setting goals and doing what it takes to achieve those goals, then you will be very successful and you will be in a position to share your success with other people, which is the most rewarding thing that you can do.

➤ Building or Re-Building Credit

For some of you bad credit isn't the issue, it's not having any credit at all. To build credit you need to use credit, therefore you have to obtain different lines of credit so that your activity will be reported to the credit bureaus.

For the rest of you, your credit isn't the best or it has taken some serious hits, and even after you pay off any collections, you will still have to open credit lines to establish new lines of credit that are reflected positively to increase your scores.

Keep in mind that every time your credit is pulled it will most likely decrease your score by a few points, so you need to be cautious about trying to open too many credit lines at once. Set your goals and try to obtain three lines of credit over a three month period. As we discussed previously, three lines of credit is optimal, less may not impact your scores enough, and if you have more than three you have to be certain that nothing gets out of hand.

In the examples for Credit Scores I listed several different ways that we used to "play the credit game." I am going to list them again for you and you will need to determine what you feel fits your budget and lifestyle the best.

- o Secured Credit Cards – If you have no credit or bad credit you may not qualify for a traditional credit card. Secured credit cards are a great alternative! For these cards you typically give the credit card company a deposit of $250 and that is the credit line that you have to use for purchases. Sometimes they will take a large fee so you may only end up with $200 for usage but as we discussed previously you shouldn't spend more than 20% of that total amount anyway. That means for a limit of $250 you should only charge $50 per month and you should always pay that in full every month.
    - There are several companies that offer secured lines of credit so look into each one and compare the fees and interest rates before you decide on the one you want to try. If it is a large company, then there is a greater chance that your secured line of credit will eventually be switched over to a traditional line of credit and that the company will give an increase to the total line of credit. The first time I used a $250 secured card, after about a year the company increased my credit line to $750 and switched the card to traditional terms.
- o Traditional Credit Cards – If you are able to qualify for a traditional term credit card then you will not be required to put down a secured deposit, the company will open a line of credit for you. Before applying for these cards contact the company to determine what

credit scores they're looking for to qualify you. If your score is too low to qualify, you don't want an inquiry, aka "a hit" to your credit for no reason.

- Installment or Personal Loans – These are tricky to come by if you have no credit or low scores. As I stated earlier, the $1000.00 "loan" that was given to my clients was put in a Savings Account and not released to the client until the loan had been paid in full. The bank charged 20% interest for those loans, so clients had to pay in $1200.00 before they were released the $1000.00. Well worth the $200.00 in my opinion to help build their scores.

Before applying for any type of loan, always ask what the qualifications are before you apply for any type of loan, again you don't want to apply for something you won't be approved for because the inquiry will lower your score and you'll have nothing to show for it.

- Furniture Payments – Most places that will finance people with no credit or lower credit scores charge high interest rates, and in some cases the furniture or electronics that they sell are priced higher than places that only lend to people with upper credit scores.
  - Be certain that they report to the credit bureaus BEFORE they pull your credit to tell you what you qualify for and before signing any paperwork.
  - Don't get carried away! Be certain that the monthly payment amount will fit your budget without putting a strain on any other area of your budget. The point is to increase your credit score, not decrease it with late payments in the event that you have stretched your budget too far. Missed payments will cause your score to drop immediately, which is the opposite of the goal!
- Car Payments – My favorite thing is to have a car paid in full! Car payments are the highest payment you will have aside from your rent/mortgage payments so absolutely make sure that you can afford the payments before you commit to buying a car that you will be financing. Again, your interest rate may be extremely high if you have no credit.

- **Refinancing!** – Always know when to refinance! A car loan will typically be for three to five years and furniture payments or installment loans will typically be for two to four years depending on the terms initially set by the contract which creates the Note or finance agreement.
    - In some cases, you can refinance after six months if your score is high enough by that point to make a difference. In most cases you're going to have to wait a year to refinance for it to be worth your effort. Keep in mind that there are always fees associated with refinancing because you're paying off the old loan by creating an entirely new account in most scenarios. Trying to refinance too soon may not be worth the fees involved.
    - Monitor your score and talk to your creditors about what is most beneficial for you before you have them try any type of refinance terms. They will have to pull your credit score again in most cases, so you don't want an inquiry on your score if you're not going to be able to refinance or the terms won't be much better than what you already have.

➢ Collections

One of the worst things for your credit aside from late payments is for debt to go to "Collections". Once debt has been sent to collections it is like having a huge red "REJECTED" stamp on your credit report. Try to negotiate to keep accounts from being sent to collections, but in most cases, creditors will not want to make any other terms aside from the original terms. I attempted to make arrangements on all seven of my credit cards, and for my reletting fee, utility bill, and cable bill, and none of the ten accounts would do anything for me, aside from turning me over to collections.

- **Negotiating New Collections** – Once a company turns you into "collections" it will either be the Collections Department within their company, or they will have "sold" your account to an outside collection agency. If it is within the original company then again, they will most likely want payment in full, or they'll want to set you up on payments. The newer the debt, the less likely they are to work with you. If you can budget the payments into your overall monthly plan, only then should you agree to the payment arrangement. If you can't, then don't stretch yourself. The account is already in collections so it's better to save up and pay the account off in full than it is to make arrangements and then default on them a second time.

o **Negotiating Old Collections** – These are the easiest to negotiate because the account could have been sold several times and once it's at a point where you can pay it off, the company you're working with may have purchased the account for much less than your original amount owed. One of the reasons why creditors won't want to work with you in the beginning is because they know they can "sell your account" to an outside collection company and make instant money off of those companies. You will no longer be their concern, as it then becomes the collection company who will be contacting you to get their investment back.

- As I stated in my Credit Score example, the original ten accounts had turned into twenty-seven on my report, so my accounts had been sold several times. Only one original creditor remained after that year and a half time period had elapsed from the accounts initially being sent to "collections."
- I did not want to get locked into another payment arrangement situation with anyone, so my strategy was to save up enough money to pay off one collection at a time. I started with the reletting fee, then the utility bill, then the cable bill, then went to the credit cards.
- If you want your credit report to look the best, then you will pay the full amount owed to your creditor to get the $0.00 and the account will reflect "Paid in Full".
- If you would rather try to negotiate a lower payoff amount, then the account will be reflected as $0.00 and will be reflected as a "Settlement".
- I'm a negotiator so I wanted to negotiate a settlement for each account that I had. None of my accounts exceeded $1,000.00, they were all between $300 - $980 so my strategy was to save

about 60% - 70% of what I owed and attempt to settle. For almost every account I followed the same script.

- Example: For an account where I owed $758, I called and stated that I wanted to settle my account. They said, "Great, the amount is $758, how will you be making that payment?"

  I replied by saying I only had $450 and that I wanted to see if I could settle for the $450 only. Their first response, "No, we can't settle for anything less than the full amount, but we can set you up on payments, can you make an initial payment of $200 now?"

  I replied by saying that I was not willing to make payments and that I had multiple other accounts in collections and that I was not going to exceed the $450. Therefore, I would simply call another company and get back to them once I had the full amount.

  Their response, "Okay, let me put you on hold and get a supervisor involved, one moment." Almost every creditor came back with a settle amount of about $100 more than what I was offering, which I had, but knew not to start with that amount. So, for that particular collection I agreed to a final "Settlement" of $550 on the $758 debt.

- Keep in mind that this will typically only work when the account has been sold to an outside company aside from the original creditor. I'm assuming they only agreed to a $550 settlement because they had paid less than that amount to buy my delinquent account to begin with. They're in the business of making money, not helping you out, so unless you give them an amount where they can still make money off of the original amount that they paid for your account they are not going to settle.

- Keep in mind that all of my accounts were reflected at $0.00 on my credit report, which did raise my scores as we discussed previously, but they were also categorized as "Settlements" instead of being "Paid in Full".

This didn't come up in conversation when I bought my home, however we have a catering company and when I was applying for our Food Truck the lender made the comment, "Our Underwriter is a little nervous about the fact that all of your old collections were settled for around 60% of what you originally owed…" Yep! 100% true!

In my mind I would have paid the original creditor 100% of what I owed them, however they didn't care enough about my circumstances and budget to work with me. They shut down the original account we had and sold it to someone else, so the original creditor already got what they wanted, and I no longer owed them anything. I was dealing with 2nd and 3rd party creditors who still made money off of the settlement agreement.

- You should do your own research on what strategy you want to go with and then make set plans and goals to tackle each issue you have on your credit report until they are all taken care of.
- I do love my free credit monitoring app and I loved watching accounts go from being all RED to now being all GREEN! Additionally, it's a great feeling to see your credit score go up each month as you get things taken care of. Again, this process could take years, but the point is to make forward conscious efforts at least once a month if possible. If you can't pay something off every month, you should be putting money in savings to build up to paying something off. Both are productive and in a forward movement towards your final goal of being debt free.

➢ Credit Repair Companies

Be extremely cautious with this area because many companies tell you that they can "consolidate your debt", and all of these great things, which simply means that they want to take over all of your debt and make you make payments to them under their terms. Those terms typically involve making you pay the full amounts and with interest added that they keep for themselves for "helping" you.

If those companies work for you then great, but those types of strategies are not for me. I preferred to leave my debt where it was and take care of every item myself one at a time, as opposed to getting locked into another payment agreement that won't initially help your credit anyway.

As I stated before, I did hire a credit repair law firm for my credit repair help. This is because for a monthly fee they helped me to dispute all items on my report that were not current, and they charge a month to month fee only. Within three months they had my report only reflecting accounts that were active and I was able to cancel the service and take over making arrangements for the debt myself.

I could have disputed all of the issues myself, but I've used this company before and I didn't know how well it would go trying to do all of that myself, or how long it would take. I knew if I let them handle it that they would do a great job and do it very quickly.

One thing I've had clients and acquaintances say about this company and about other companies like this is, "They didn't work, there is still stuff on my credit report!" My response, "Correct because you still owe that money!" You don't use credit repair companies with the thought process that they're magicians that are going to magically erase your debt, that's not going to happen. You use them to clean up issues on your report that are old and in need of attention.

I've also heard and seen this, "They don't work because stuff was taken off of my report and then a month or two later it was put back on!" Correct again! That is because when a dispute occurs the creditor has thirty days to prove that you owe the debt, or the debt has to be removed from your report. However, if they get around to "proving" that you owe the debt ninety days later then they can report the debt again and it will be put back on.

If you owe money to a creditor then you owe money, end of story. The only thing to negotiate is how you pay them that money, the debt is never going to go away. If your first thought is, "Shouldn't it fall off of my report after seven years?", my response to you is that if you set goals for yourself you can get it off yourself in half that time or less.

Being in debt should be for a season, not for a lifetime.

➢ Bankruptcy

When most people get into financial difficulties their initial response is to file bankruptcy. By doing this you will have years that follow where you will have to be placed in a category where the creation of new debt is almost non-existent, therefore everything you do will have to be paid for with cash, or not at all. If you are able to make plans to pay off debt yourself within a few years, then I can promise you that collections (that you eventually take care of) look much better than a bankruptcy, which is credit that you did not take care of.

This personal story represents the second time I went through complete financial ruin. The first time was in 2007 and was due to the fact that my son had Leukemia and was ill to the point that I was unable to work because there was no one to care for him but me. At that time, I was a single parent working for a builder in Dallas and I owned a home, and two cars that were all financed in my name only. I was only a couple of years into my career and did not have the knowledge of credit and credit options that I have gained over the last decade, so I did what most people do and filed bankruptcy. I surrendered my home and one of my cars so that I would not have a Foreclosure or a repossession on my credit report.

After filing bankruptcy, I then moved back to Amarillo where I was able to get nursing care for my son and continue with my career. To repair my credit from bankruptcy status I followed the same steps that I've given you previously. So, within a three year period I was able to get a secured credit card and finance a vehicle, which eventually took my score from the low 500's up to an over 750+ which is where it stayed until this second scenario kicked in.

While I would keep bankruptcy as a last resort, I was able to overcome the aftermath in the same manner we've been talking about. If you have a home, multiple vehicles, credit cards that are into five figures, etc., then you may need to look into this option. My suggestion to you before making your final decision is to research every available option before making the final commitment, because once it is filed, you will be required to disclose it repeatedly and it will affect every area of your life including, applications for rental property for several years.

No matter what happens to your credit, there is always a way back to having a positive credit report. When you're in the moment of financial ruin and dealing with it every day, life can be a serious struggle. The key is to make a plan to get out. A literal escape plan! We've covered multiple ways to trim your budget, ways to fix items on your credit report, and we will discuss multiple ways to add to your budget with MSI's in the Personal Goals section. All of the goals and plans that you create will set you up for success. Your credit issues will be for a season that may last multiple years, however once you get started, you will solidify the fact that credit problems will not last a lifetime.

Debt Repayment Plan

After your budget is finalized and you have determined the exact amount that you will have each month in excess of your fixed budget, you are then able to begin creating a plan for the repayment of your debt. This will include any credit card debt, past debt unrelated to your current expenses, as well as any debt that has been sent to collections.

By strategically planning the repayment of your debt you will be able to determine when your credit scores will reflect a positive number. This will enable you to plan personal goals for things involving the necessity of having a positive credit score to obtain financing or to be approved for housing and other life choices that revolve around qualifications based on your credit score.

Determine the portion of the overage from your fixed budget that you will be able to use for debt repayment. It must be an amount that does not interfere with your fixed budget or with the amount needed to maintain a comfortable level in your bank account between paydays. Determine the exact amount that you can allocate to debt repayment after all monthly expenses are paid in full.

Current Debt Breakdown
- Past Bills (previous residence) = $_____
- Credit Card debt = $_____
- Collections = $_____

- _____ = $_____
- _____ = $_____
- _____ = $_____
- **Total of all Debt = $_____**

Take the total amount of debt and divide it by the monthly amount allocated for your debt repayment plan. The answer will equal the amount of months it will take you to pay your debt in full:

$_____ = Total of all Debt
/ $_____ = Monthly amount allocated for debt repayment
= _____ = Total amount of months it will take to repay the total debt

As discussed in the "Collections" section, if the monthly amount isn't enough to pay one unit of debt in full, then an optimal option is to save the monthly amount until you have the total amount needed to pay off one unit completely. This can either be as either a "settlement" or "paid in full" status.

By paying off one debt in full your credit score will rise slightly once the repayment has posted to the credit bureaus. Keep in mind that it may take up to six weeks for a fully paid debt to reflect as being paid per the credit bureaus. In most cases you must pay off a debt between the $1^{st} - 14^{th}$ in order for the payment to be reflected as paid the following month. Payments made on the 15th – end of the month may take up to six weeks to be reflected as paid in full.

If the total amount of months to repay your debt is discouraging, use the Personal Goals section regarding creating MSI (Multiple Sources of Income). When you have a set budget with your current monthly income, then the money from your MSI can be used towards your debt repayment which will decrease the amount of months you initially determined.

The average for most people to repay debt less than $10,000 is 36 – 60 months or 3 – 5 years. Although a plan that will take years may seem discouraging, the sooner you begin the sooner the debt will be repaid. Create a plan that is optimal for your budget, implement it immediately, and do not deviate from the plan.

You determine your own rate of success and success begins when you take action towards your final goal.

Personal Goals

Alright, now you've come a long way! You have used the Workbook to create a budget that will make your lifestyle predictable, which may not be overly comfortable, but it is livable. So, it's time now to look at where you stand. You put yourself on The Divorce Diet, the question is, how's it going? Do you feel like you're fasting, and you want to get off the diet and back to eating steaks for breakfast, or are you feeling great about your diet and you feel like you'll be set if you continue on the course that you're on?

Once again, the great thing about life is that you get out of it what you put into it. Therefore, if you're happy where you're at, then good for you! You can continue to maintain your lifestyle and set personal goals for things that you like to do instead of focusing on setting goals for obtaining more income and getting "off the diet". On the other hand, if you're not a huge fan of the diet you've put yourself on, all you have to do is determine what you need to do to obtain your goals so that you can get what you want out of life.

For those of you that are not happy with your current situation, the question now is, how do you create more income and get back to where you were, or get to a point that you will feel that you are financially free to do what you want to do in life?

Now is the time to think about where you want to be. Focus on where you want to be. Literally stop reading this and for thirty minutes, sit quietly without any outside influence of TV, music, (potentially 30 minutes without the sound of children may be impossible right this second, but if so, then do it after they are asleep!) and think about what your financial situation, living arrangements, and occupation would be like if you could do anything you want, be anything you want.

Guess what? I'm here to tell you that you can do anything you want, and you can be anything you want. If you don't think that's true, then who told you that? Your ex-spouse that is no longer around to tell you what to do? Perhaps your parents were the type to tell you that dreaming gets you nowhere and that dreams don't pay the bills? Maybe a boss or co-workers have laughed or scoffed at goals that you've set for yourself? If you don't have supportive friends keep in mind that misery loves company, what type of company are you keeping?

My next question to you is this, why are you letting other people determine who you are? Only you truly know who you are, and honestly most of us don't even know that simply because we look to others for validation of ourselves. What a sad way to live!

This is your time now! Your time to figure out who you are and what you want out of life. The only person that can stop you, is you! One of the main reasons that people don't reach their goals is that they don't even set goals. They have a dream or a wish and all they ever do is say, "If only I could…" without ever making the plans to move towards that goal.

My goal of moving to Colorado was to further my writing career by becoming a screenwriter with the ultimate goal of also becoming a producer and director. After moving here and focusing on my writing I was able to put two of my novels into screenplays, write a children's book about my son, begin giving presentations, and everything else I had dreamed of doing.

My life was going great in that I had paired up with a producer from L.A. who had loved both of my scripts (which are based on my novels *CIRCUMSTANTIAL* and *Times Three*). We had two Option Agreements and he had told me all of the wonderful things that would be happening once he was able to lock in the funding for the films. In addition, he promised me an internship with the director, and I was absolutely willing to work for free with a director as many times as possible knowing that I would need that knowledge before ever trying to direct anything myself.

He "passed" on multiple offers for a $5 million dollar budget because he believed that he could "lock in" a $20 million budget for *CIRCUMSTANTIAL* and a $40 million budget for *Times Three*. I know that sounds like a lot but if you look up your favorite movie on IMBD the cost of the film was most likely triple that and then some. He considered the $5 million offer to be "low-budget" and he believed my scripts were worth more.

A screenwriter typically gets 5% of the total budget so I would have been very happy with the $250,000 that he passed on, but as the writer I have zero say in the situation. I trusted him that he would be able to handle everything and admittedly being paid $3,000,000 if he was able to get his full $60,000,000 for both films sounded amazing!! I fully believed that he would come through on everything that he had promised.

What did my ex think about all of these great things that were happening?? He hated it! When I told him that I was going to Portland, OR for eight weeks to film *Times Three* he completely lost it. My "goals and dreams" were great while they were imaginary, however when the reality of reaching those goals began to set it, my "family" lifestyle unraveled very quickly. I suppose I should admit that we were already divorced when we moved to Colorado so that was a second attempt for our marriage, which also ended in failure.

My producer wanted to play the lead role in *Times Three* and use it as his "break" to go from producer to actor. Eventually he called me to say that he didn't have enough acting credits per the film company to play the lead, so he once again "passed" on their offer, and he was going to "hold onto" my scripts until he had more credits. That was the beginning of a huge disappointing ride.

To make a very long story short the point is…what do I have to show for all of that?? Well, I have Option Agreements with the producer, a Submission Agreement between him and one of the leading film companies in the industry, and I have my two scripts showing as being in the "Project in development" stage on IMDB, all of which have no monetary value, so none of those things can be taken to the bank and deposited.

My son has special needs and they told me it would take 30 days to set up his care. I thought 30 days was plenty of time to get things under control and nothing would be a problem so I left my ex thinking we would struggle for a month at most. It actually took a year and a half due to the mishandling of paperwork and turn over within the agency that handled the process. As parents with special needs children can tell you, you can't leave them home by themselves, and you can't take them to work with you.

Therefore, if you can't make money at home and you don't have assistance for their care, you are in a very serious situation.

I left my ex thinking that I would have six or seven figures in the bank within a few months, to the realization that I was about to be on a very serious, very devasting, ride to the bottom.

I became emotionally and financially devastated. I had no energy to try and find another producer, I simply had to go into survival mode and do all of the things that we've talked about to get myself back on track. I needed some serious motivation to keep my head up. It absolutely helped that every time I went outside, I was able to see the Rocky Mountains, but I had to put in time and effort to keep myself motivated so that I would stay positive for myself and for my son.

If you're the type to listen to music, then unfortunately you probably associate many songs with instances that occurred with other people. Being from Texas, admittedly I do love country music. I love it because contrary to popular belief, it's not about your dog dying, it instead focuses on family and most of the songs are related to family gatherings, and how family interacts with one another, and are positive in nature. Well, after I left my ex the last thing I wanted to hear was family related songs. So, I tried to go back to listening to other types of music, which typically relate to going out to have a great time and meeting someone, which I couldn't afford to do nor did I want to do, or the lyrics talk about one person cheating on another, and if only they could get another chance. Hmm, not helping either. So now what?

I started researching motivational speakers and material to listen to. As most of us know, anything you could possibly think of is on YouTube so if you have internet access, then you have access to any type of information you want. When I started searching for motivational speakers, I was surprised to come across several celebrities that were talking about their personal stories. Since they're celebrities we look at them with the thought that they're "special" and that there is something different about them. They must have had a special upbringing, or they must have known someone in the industry to help them, they must have had money to help them get the best training, etc. The reality of most of their situations is exactly the opposite.

Who do you admire? Who do you think is a person that you respect enough to look into their background, into their life story? I'm guessing that once you look into it you will find that they came from a challenging background and that they failed more times than they've ever achieved things. The difference between them and you is their actions and the fact that they set goals for themselves to overcome their fear of failure. Most importantly, they never gave up or stopped reaching for their goals and dreams.

In addition to writing books, as discussed previously, I write screenplays and anytime I'm fearful of being rejected for a project I envision a room full of actors all going in to audition for the same part. Every single one of them is told no, except for the one who makes it. For those that were told no, do you think they went home and cried, and never tried again? Possible, but doubtful. They had to shake it off and try again. And for the actor that actually got the part, do you think that was the first time that they ever auditioned for a part? Also doubtful. How many times do you think they heard the word no, before finally hearing the word yes?

The same can be said for anyone in the music industry, models, athletes, writers, inventors, and literally for any successful person. The fear of failure and of hearing the word "no" is what keeps most people from greatness. In my initial sales training for selling new homes the statistics were that for every ten times you ask for a sale, you will only close one. So, you have to be diligent enough to get through the nine rejections to get to that one "yes". Those individuals strong enough to believe in themselves and to view every "no" or every "failure" as a stepping stone to greatness always make it in the end. The key is to keep going. NEVER STOP!

I have a children's book entitled *My Friend Gavin* which is about my youngest son who has Down Syndrome and who is also a Leukemia survivor. When I read this book for presentations to children, I always like to take time to talk to them about striving to do the things that they're dreaming for. Most people, including children, are familiar with the concept of people not supporting your dreams, but what happens when they do?

I love to use two examples, two of my favorite stories. The first, is Alice in Wonderland. Alice goes into Wonderland and is told that she is there to save that realm from the Jabberwocky. Everyone believes that she has the ability to slay the Jabberwocky and save everyone. The problem of the story is that Alice does not believe in herself. She thinks everyone is "mad" and that surely there is a mistake, she can't possibly slay a Jabberwocky to save the day, she's never done that before! As the story progresses Alice is put in situations that show her that she is actually capable of more than she thinks, and when she finally believes in herself, she is able to overcome her fear, accept who she is, and slay the Jabberwocky!

The second story is The Matrix. Ironically there is a play on Alice in Wonderland by having Neo "Follow the white rabbit", and when he's asked if he wants to take the red pill or the blue pill. Once Neo decides to take the red pill and "stay in Wonderland to see how deep the rabbit hole goes", he learns that everyone believes that he is the "One" and that he has the ability to save what is left of the human race. Once again, he thinks there must be a mistake, he's never saved anyone before, there's nothing special about him aside from the fact that he's a great hacker, right? Again, things happen that show him that he's more capable than he thinks he is. And only when he begins to believe in himself, does he realize that he truly is the "One" and he's able to not only bend, but break every rule of The Matrix to save his people.

It doesn't matter how many people believe in you if you don't first believe in yourself. If you're the only person that believes in you, then you win, because that's all you need to be successful! Once you have a belief system down, then you have to begin taking the steps to obtain greatness. One step at a time, always in forward progression.

One motivational speaker I listen to said, "The difference between a wish and a dream, is that a wish is something that you speak of, yet never truly expect to happen. A dream is something that you have to work towards. As Jesus said, 'Faith without works is dead'." – JO

If reaching our goals and achieving our dreams were easy, then everyone would do it. It's much easier to show up to a place and let another person tell you what to do, then come home and watch other successful people on TV that you can relate to and live vicariously through. This is what most people do, and if that makes you happy, then good for you, but if it doesn't, then what are you going to do about it? Set goals and work towards them, that's what!

Some of you may be thinking, I'm not trying to be famous, I'm just trying to be able to live comfortably. Well, since you're in the situation of not living comfortably then you can now see that in order to get back to that level, you have to set goals and you have to work towards them. Expecting someone to knock on your door and tell you that all of your problems are solved is most likely not going to happen. You have to make the personal and physical effort to get yourself where you want to be.

For all of us, regardless of our gender, race, social class, background, or dreams, we all have the same goal = happiness! Some people think they'll be happy when they can live in a big city and live and shop as they please, while others would find happiness by being in a remote country setting with no one around and nothing to spend money on. Being happy is individualized to each of us, so to begin the process of goal setting, you must first determine what will make YOU happy, not what everyone else expects you to do so that you can be "successful" in their eyes.

Earlier I talked about sitting quietly for 30 minutes to determine what would make you happy. That seems like such a simple concept, however most people never take the time to sit quietly and "think". Instead they either have the TV, radio, book, social media, games, or other things telling them what to think in that moment. Time is precious and valuable, just like you need to pay attention to your financial budget, you also need to pay attention to your time management.

Most people think that meditation relates to burning incense, sitting cross legged, and going through certain rituals. This may be true for some people, but ultimately meditation is simply sitting quietly with your own thoughts. When you do the research on successful people that we talked about, you're going to find that most of them, if not all of them, take time to be by themselves with their thoughts. All of them imagined who they wanted to become, and they began to have a thought process that entertained how their life would be once they achieved their goal. They imagined what they would be doing, how they would be dressed, where they would live, how much money would be in their accounts, who they would be surrounded by, what they would do for entertainment, and everything else associated with the lifestyle they wanted to achieve. Most importantly, they thought about how that new lifestyle would make them feel.

There are so many examples of amazing people that achieved greatness that I could write a book on that alone, instead, I'll simply name a few. Einstein stated that his thought process was comprised of sitting quietly at his desk by himself and that thoughts would come to him or be channeled through him. "Imagination is everything. It is the preview to life's coming attractions." – Albert Einstein. Earl Nightingale has a 30 minute YouTube recording called "The Strangest Secret by Earl Nightingale" in which he talks about the fact that the "secret" is to sit and "think". He states that the problem with most unsuccessful people is that "they simply don't think".

Most people are familiar with the book and documentary called "The Secret" where Rhonda Byrne interviewed multiple people who practice the Law of Attraction. All of them will tell you that success comes down to your own personal thought processes. That documentary was based on book *The Science of Getting Rich*, and another similar book is *Think and Grow Rich*. In addition to those books, almost everyone in the documentary "The Secret" has written books on the same subject, using your thought processes to gain success and live an abundant lifestyle.

As I said earlier, you get out of life what you put into it. If what you're putting into your life is watching TV shows full of drama, then guess what, you're probably going to feel and live with lots of drama. If you constantly immerse yourself with social media, then guess what, you're probably going to feel anxious and be focused on things that are not related to your intended goal.

Most of us work for other people for at least 40 hours per week, which means that your own personal time is limited, and it is very precious. If you're wanting to get more out of life, then set a goal to use the personal time that you have to fill yourself with motivational information that will help you achieve your goals.

Setting and Obtaining Personal Goals

Once you've determined what you want to do, you then have to set goals to do it. If what you want is to be more successful in a certain field, then most likely you are going to have to determine how to obtain the education or the training to reach the level you are trying to achieve.

Luckily, we live in a time where we can obtain education and accreditation through an online University so that we are able to continue working which is necessary to have the income needed for your financial responsibilities. If you're thinking that you work all day and that the last thing you want to do in the evening and on the weekends is school work, then I hope that you're comfortable at the level you're at. If you want something bad enough, you will use that "time management" that we talked about to spend time educating yourself, instead of watching other people in whatever show would typically take up that time.

If your goal is not to further your education, but to achieve your dream of being in a certain field, then research what it takes to achieve that goal and structure your time so that you can make forward progress to get there.

If you don't want to further your education, and you don't want to reach a "dream" and your main concern is simply how to make more money with your current situation, then my question to you is, what is your talent? You may be thinking that if you were talented then you'd be trying to do one of the other situations listed above, however that's not always true. Everyone is talented whether you have tapped into it or not.

MSI's or Multiple Sources of Income

If you have limited income, yet want to create more income for yourself, then ask yourself what you can do for others that they would in turn give you money for. If you were to read the book or listen to the audiobook of *The Science of Getting Rich* then you will learn that success and the achievement of money, is an exchange. You give something first, then receive money second. That concept is confusing for most people because we're used to simply exchanging our time for money, however if you tap into your "talents" then you will see that by using those talents you have something to give to people, and that they will repay you for your talent with money. Can you take great pictures, can you paint, can you draw, can you cook, can you clean, can you do landscaping? You can use any of those talents to set goals that will allow you to share those talents with others in exchange for money.

Research the business laws in your area for the things that you like to do. Colorado has a "Cottage Law" that will allow you to prepare certain foods in your home that are "non-potentially hazardous" that you can sell at Farmer's Markets and other areas based on the restrictions within that county. If you want to start a cleaning or landscaping service, determine if you have to obtain a license or if you can simply market yourself for those services.

Several churches may allow you to advertise in their weekly fliers for services that you can provide to their members. Some elderly members may not have the ability to clean their own home and keep up with their landscaping, or to pay for traditional companies that market in their area. If you can provide the service at a price they can afford, this might be an optimal situation to make additional money.

If you live in a beautiful place such as Colorado, then you can take nature photographs and sell them at a local flea market. There are booths for paintings and drawings as well. You can pretty much sell anything at a flea market and most places of that nature will let you rent a booth for less than $100, some even for around $40 for the weekend. Refurbished old used furniture made into something new and beautiful is something that many people love to buy these days. Buy something from a yard sale that is tragic, then redo it into something new and wonderful.

Structure your budget to allow you to spend a little bit of money, to turn around and make double or triple that money. The ways in which you can make money are endless if you simply research doing what you love to do. Invest in yourself and you'll be amazed at what you can achieve.

Once you have determined what you want your personal goal to be, you must map it out in the same way that you budget your finances. You have to determine what it's going to take to get you where you need to be, then map it out on a calendar as if it were a literal map to your life. View every day as if you are walking towards that final goal and make certain that you do something every day to work towards obtaining it, even if the daily activity is simply "thinking" about it. I highly recommend taking 30 minutes every morning to visualize and think about your goal and how you will feel once you've obtained it. "Feeling the feeling" of success is something that you will hear repeatedly when you research the processes of successful people.

All of these options mentioned can turn from a small business venture into business ownership where you are able to begin working for yourself full time. One more very important part of all of this great new income...always pay attention to tax laws when creating additional income for yourself!!

The "Process"

In this day and age, and especially if you're in your 20's, you love instant gratification, and the thought of your goal taking years to achieve can seem extremely overwhelming. While this is true, if you don't start taking the steps towards those goals today, then you are simply prolonging the process, and five years will turn into six, which will turn into seven, and before you know it, you've lived a decade on a diet that was only meant to last for a few years.

When you're feeling discouraged and the word "failure" keeps coming to mind, remember this - "Failure is an event, it's not who you are," – JO.

Once you start the process of setting a goal, and then you begin taking steps to obtain that goal, I can promise you that goal setting will become addictive and it will become a life practice. You will realize that once you reach a certain level, you're excited that you've achieved that level, but what's next? I like to think about it in reference to climbing a mountain. You go up one trail and you reach the end and you're at a beautiful clearing. You've made it to the end and that's exciting, but you look around and think how do you get higher? You then search for another trail and you keep going. Then once you've reached the top of that mountain you look over and see that there is another mountain, and another. Why stop at one mountain when you can conquer them all?

In the same presentation where I talked to the kids about Alice in Wonderland and The Matrix, I also talked to them about the fact that once you've reached a goal, you're still never finished! Most of them looked at me like I was crazy, which does happen a lot I should say, so I had to give them examples.

I was at an Elementary School in Littleton, CO where my son Gavin was in 6th grade at the time. I was speaking to the entire school which was broken into two different sessions, Kindergarten – 3rd grade, followed by 4th grade – 6th grade. I asked both groups to choose a male athlete that was their favorite and to pick a female singer that was their favorite. Ironically, both groups picked the same two people; Peyton Manning who was the Quarterback for the Broncos at that time; and Katy Perry who I am assuming all of you know very well.

For the K – 3rd grade group I asked them if they thought that there were people that discouraged either of those two celebrities by talking badly about them. This first group looked mortified that I would even say such a thing. Who would talk badly about Peyton Manning or Katy Perry? Surely this isn't happening! What was I possibly talking about? Since I'm a Psychology major and fan of people watching in general, I found this to be very interesting. This group still had the thought process that once you were a celebrity then all of life had to be grand and fairytale like. It's nice to know that some children still believe this to be true and I wish that both groups had the same response, however that wasn't the case.

The second group of 4th – 6th graders was asked the same question. One boy in the front yelled, "My Dad says Peyton Manning sucks!" In addition, a girl in the back yelled, "My Mom hates Katy Perry!" Interesting that the kids weren't sharing their own personal opinions, but they were sharing the opinion of their parents who had apparently been very vocal about what they thought of those celebrities.

My next question to the groups were, "How has the opinion of people that don't like Peyton Manning and Katy Perry affected those two?" Again, I got looks of wonderment.... I continued by saying, "I don't think that the fact that someone's Dad thinking that Peyton Manning sucks, or that someone's Mom doesn't like Katy Perry has stopped either one of them from achieving greatness, do you?"

Unfortunately, I had to break it to the little ones that there are a ton of people on social media that say negative things about both celebrities, while the second group was obviously well aware of this. One thing that both groups knew very well, was that Peyton Manning was able to achieve greatness with two different NFL teams, and that Katy Perry is an international superstar regardless of what is being said about them negatively by anyone.

My point to the kids, and to you, is that if you think that you need the approval of others to achieve greatness, then you're going to be disappointed. If you base everything you do off of the opinion of other people, then you're not going to get very far. What other people say about you is irrelevant if you are being true to yourself. You will NEVER be able to make everyone happy, therefore the goal should be to make YOURSELF happy.

Another question I asked is this, "Since Peyton was so good that he was able to win a Superbowl, does that mean that he gets to skip practice and just show up for games?" This one made both groups quiet.... Hmm, he is one of the great Quarterbacks so, what does that mean? Can he?

Additionally, "Since Katy Perry is a world superstar, does that mean that she never has to practice her songs or routines before a show?" Quiet again... She's amazing, never skips a beat, can sing and dance simultaneously while looking astonishing, surely all of that comes naturally, and in the moment, right?

My point there for both celebrities and for anyone that achieves greatness, is that no matter how great you get, you can never stop practicing or sharpening your skills, NEVER! So, if you set goals with the mindset that once one is achieved then you can just sit back and relax, you have a misconception of what it takes to stay on point once your goals have been achieved.

If you've never set goals for yourself before and you're feeling overwhelmed, you shouldn't. The fact that you've read this far into this book, and the fact that you even bought this book in the first place, tells me that you're the type of person to want to have forward progress. You started the process by buying this book, which I assume was intended to help you figure out ways to overcome financial difficulties associated with divorce. Figuring out what you want next out of life, and setting goals for yourself, is going to come more naturally to you than you think.

Take the time now to write out where you want to be in five years. Once you've done that, research what it will take to get there. Once you've done that, start mapping out your steps on the calendar to set serious goals for yourself to get where you want to be, in the timeframe that you want to be there.

Once again, Alice or Neo, you can do and achieve anything you want, you only have to believe in yourself first.

Lifestyle Changes

Now that you're on a serious diet, you will most likely have to make some lifestyle changes to stay on point with your budget and with your goals. Some of you may feel like the word "fun" is now non-existent and that your life is full of restrictions. If your idea of "fun" previously was spending money for shopping or entertainment, you now have to look for new ways to have "fun". It is important for you and for your children to stay positive and to look for new opportunities. The best way to start is to look for different places and programs in your community that offer "fun" for free.

Most places have a multitude of parks that are free to visit. If you haven't spent time kicking a ball with your children in the park, then you're missing out on some serious fun. It's amazing how the most simple things can create laughter and happiness for your family.

If you don't have kids, then you can still go to a park or a small pond or lake with a track around it and walk to enjoy the scenery and to have those quiet moments to yourself that we've been talking about. I can't think of anything more productive than walking while in a nature setting. If you think that trees don't talk, then I'm positive that you've never been on a trail by yourself surrounded only by trees. Enjoy listening to the trees, I promise you, that they will talk to you. The only thing you should do with your phone, is to take pictures! Not only is walking in nature great for you, bringing home pictures of those beautiful trees, flowers, water, and of the birds that followed you while you walk, will help you have a little piece of happiness with you.

If you were used to going to do something fun and completed the day by eating out, then pack a lunch to take with you so that you can still "eat out". Most parks have picnic tables, and even if they don't, take a blanket or towels and enjoy sitting outside and eating together.

My favorite thing about living in Colorado is that we've lived here for four and a half years now, and we still haven't done everything outdoors that there is to do for free. There are endless amounts of mountain trails that are free, and we love to try new trails all the time. The only thing that costs money here (aside from large tourist attractions) is a $7 entry fee (per vehicle, not per person) for National Parks, which is well worth it! The National Parks here are amazing and if you love taking pictures of beautiful scenery, then you will never be disappointed.

Do you have bicycles? If not, buying some bikes new or used is a small expense compared to shopping and eating out every weekend. Biking together is not only a fun activity, but it is also great exercise, something that many of us don't get enough of.

Research libraries in your area. Libraries typically have something free going on every weekend. In addition to the free activity you can rent books and movies both from libraries. Taking a weekly trip to the library is a wonderful thing for you to do alone, or as a family. In most cases, there is not a fee associated with anything that you can do there.

Did your life prior to going on this diet include a gym membership that you can no longer afford? Whether you "paid" to exercise previously, or you simply want to get in shape but think you can't afford it, I promise you that you can get in great shape for free!

Anytime I hear someone say, "I would be in great shape if I could afford a gym membership", I'm positive that person has never gotten in their living room floor and tried to do push-ups. I can promise you that your own body weight is plenty! You don't need extra weights to get into shape, use your own body weight with certain exercises and you'll find out very quickly that you've been missing out on a great workout this entire time.

There are a ton of Yoga videos for $10 or less available at stores. If you think that Yoga wouldn't get you into shape, then again, you've obviously never tried it. You don't need large gym equipment to get into shape, you need the knowledge of how to use your own body weight to your advantage.

One day my mother came into my living room and I was streaming music videos on my TV through YouTube, and I was doing squats to the music. She said, "What are you doing?", to which I replied, "My Justin Bieber workout!" If you try and do 100 squats then that can seem daunting, however if you simply do squats to your favorite songs then you'll be squatting for about 2 – 3 minutes, which is actually more than 100 repetitions. Have you looked at the body of dancers? Their legs are amazing because it takes some serious leg muscles to keep up that level of dancing. Simply dancing to music is a great workout and you can do this by yourself, or with your kids. It doesn't matter if you can dance well because you're in your living room, and the point is that you're moving, not trying to impress anyone. Always dance like no one is watching and have a great time!

Again, Pinterest is an excellent place to search for workout routines that you can do at home for free. You can find workout schedules, and specific workouts for legs, arms, abs, and anything else you can think of.

In the past four years I feel like I've been able to stay in pretty good shape and the only money I've spent is $150 on a treadmill. The best time to buy a treadmill is after April. Lots of people buy treadmills with the intention of using them, however they become bulky coat racks, or sit there collecting dust. April is about the time that people realize that they're not going to use them, and they just want them out of the way.

I had saved $150 for a treadmill and was determined to find one for that amount. I ended up finding one for that exact price at a Play It Again Sports store. It looked like it had never been used, but it was definitely huge! I brought it home and put it in my living room right in front of my TV. It took up the entire space and we literally had to walk around it to get from the living room to the kitchen, but I didn't care. That was part of my "gym" and it was staying in place.

Walking while watching TV is multi-tasking in my mind and a great way to keep your mind off the fact that you're working out. My favorite thing to watch while walking is the motivational videos that I was talking about earlier. Listening to someone talk about achieving their goals while walking on my treadmill made me feel like I was tackling two goals at once, which is great for your mindset.

Admittedly, another thing I like to stream as I walk is videos of Victoria's Secret runway shows! Beautiful women strutting down the runway to great music, and live performances, love it! Let me tell you what happens when you hit your 40's, gravity kicks in that's what! Parts of your body that were previously in one place, start slipping south with the gravitational pull of the Universe. I'm not a fan of looking in the mirror, but I am a fan of watching other beautiful women. Remember my earlier statements of watching TV to live vicariously through others, in this case, I'm guilty, but at least I'm working out while watching them!

Changes with Friends & Family

As stated previously, if you were in the routine of going out with friends and family to spend money, and now you are no longer able to spend that money, you will be faced with the fact that your relationships with those people may change.

Unfortunately, you can't expect other people to stop spending money and doing what they like to do, simply because you can no longer afford to do it. Don't make the mistake of getting bitter because others won't be excited about your new "free" lifestyle. Once again, other people don't define who you are, you determine that yourself.

We've talked about many things that are hard to deal with psychologically, and this is one of the hardest. You lost your spouse, and now you may also lose friends, and events previously done with family members because you are no longer able to afford doing those things.

While this can be devastating to some people, embrace this as your opportunity to find yourself. We've been talking about self-reflection and figuring out who you are as an individual, well, you can't do that if you're always surrounded by other people.

This is a conversation that you're also going to have to have with your children if they are used to going to the mall, going to the movies, or doing other things with their friends that they can no longer do. Explain to them the same things that I've been explaining to you. Some of the people that they admire the most were "loners" as kids. Outcasts that didn't "fit in" with the popular crowd. Ironic that many outcasts set trends that popular kids follow, but that's the key, the separation of the leader and the follower. Hopefully your children can also learn to find a new side of themselves and start to enjoy things as individuals that they didn't know they liked to do.

Have you or your children ever tried to write, paint, or draw? In the current world of technology, the process of "creation" seems to be a side note. Most writers can tell you that writing starts with a thought process, followed by writing down thoughts in a journal or composition book, and only after that process is completed are the words transferred onto a typed platform. I have my composition book where I outlined this entire book sitting next to me right now. People tell me all the time, "I've thought about writing but I don't know where to start." Well, I just told you where to start, and a composition book costs about $1, so if writing is something that you're interested in, then the time to get started is now.

People get "writer's block" because they think that they're going to write their final draft with their first draft. Not likely! Purge any ideas you have into that composition book, then rearrange them in your mind, then label the new arrangement, then get started. You will most likely have multiple drafts of anything you write so never be afraid to start or be afraid that anything will be written "wrong". There's no such thing. And ALWAYS write for yourself! As we talked about previously, you'll never be able to write a short story, poem, song, or book that everyone will like. There will always be someone who doesn't like it, so the important thing to remember is that YOU need to like it. That's all that matters.

I've always wanted to be a painter but putting family first caused me to put painting on the side and I never tried. One of the very first things I spent money on when I was able to begin spending a little money, was on painting supplies. There are two main craft stores in almost every area, and both will put art supplies on sale for 50% off at least one weekend a month, if not more. Spending little bits of money at a time allowed me to build up quite the art supply collection and today my granddaughters both have paintings hanging in their rooms that I've painted, and my 16-year-old son is quite the artist! He has about ten dinosaur paintings that he's done which are hanging in his room that he's quite proud of.

As my friend Bob Ross would say, "You can't tell a painting how to be." Which means, there's no such thing as not being able to paint. If you have

Hulu, then several seasons of Bob Ross Painting are available to stream!! Super exciting!

If you're thinking that you can't paint landscape pictures, or don't want to, look up some pictures of Picasso paintings and I'm guessing that you'll figure out that you can paint however you want to paint. There's no such thing as how a painting is "supposed" to look.

The same can be said for drawing and drawing supplies. If you or your children would love to start drawing, then you should begin looking into buying sketch books and artist pencils or markers so that you can begin to express yourself in that way. Nothing has to be perfect, you simply just have to draw what you feel.

Since I am a writer the thought of not being able to put my emotions on paper is a traumatizing thought. When I lived in Texas and was a Realtor I also volunteered as a Rape Crisis Advocate and I was a Respite worker for the Domestic Violence shelter. When I started working at the shelter I asked if they had any journals or composition books to give to the women and children as they came in. The answer, was no. What?!? I would spontaneously combust if I was unable to get my rage, anxiety, and other emotions out of my body and onto paper in some way.

The next time I went to the shelter I took a bag of composition books and several packs of pens. It cost me less than $30 and I knew that amount was nothing compared to the priceless process of being about to put your emotions on paper to deal with them. Keeping emotions internalized is similar to a pressure cooker. If that pressure isn't released correctly, there can absolutely be an explosion that follows.

For those of you who are thinking that you don't like to write about your feelings or keep a "diary", I'm the same way. I make up fictional stories and characters to act out my emotions for me instead of putting myself through a pity party of emotional distress. My two main published fictional works and their screenplays are dark thrillers, so I have to admit that I'm quite talented at being violent on paper, while in reality I do my best to keep that side of myself under control.

Going through a divorce is hurtful to everyone involved and if you can find an outlet of expression for yourself and for your children then it will help you get through it in a productive manner.

Do What You Love

You've been doing all of this self-reflection to figure out who you are and what you enjoy. Once you figure it out be sure to do what you love! Even though I did love real estate, I'm a writer! I've been writing since I was 8 years old and I spent decades in unrelated fields to make money to make other people happy. I conformed with society to have a "reputable career".

When I split with my ex all of my family expected me to return to Texas because he did. Well, I'm not him, and even though my son and I went through some serious financial hardships to stay in Colorado it didn't matter. I moved here to focus on my writing because that is my love and my passion, and I refused to let anyone try to take that from me.

For me there is something magical about the mountains. I was born in Texas, but I also lived in both West Virginia and Missouri as a child and my favorite thing to do was play in the woods! Being able to look at the Rocky Mountains every day makes me feel extremely wealthy and that I'm in the presence of greatness. Hiking in the Rocky Mountains is more spiritually motivating than I can put into words, and I'm a writer, so there you have it.

We've been talking about achieving great goals which come with great monetary rewards also, but if you're happy living in a small space with a little garden in the window and reading books you love every day, then do that! The amount of money you have isn't going to equate to your happiness in most circumstances. You can be happy with a small amount of money as long as you're doing what you love to do.

If you work in an industry that makes you unhappy, then change that by setting goals to spend your time doing what you love. As long as you FEEL wealthy, then you will be. There are plenty of miserable people with a lot of money in their bank accounts. Don't make the mistake of thinking that happiness only equals money. Most of the things that make us the happiest can't be bought with money.

One motivational speaker I listen to talks about the fact that most people don't want to be millionaires, they simply want to be able to obtain whatever they want in that moment. Even if you have millions in the bank you will only use what you need each day for food, transportation, shopping, entertainment, and shelter. So, if you can obtain the resources to do what you love every day, then in essence, you are a millionaire - BP.

"Indoor Camping"

When we were living in a manner that was devasting and the opposite of how we were used to living, I told myself and my son that we were simply "Indoor Camping". When you go camping you take the bare essentials and leave all of the comforts of home behind.

This is a great way to train your brain to understand that all of the extra things that you're used to having aren't absolutely necessary like you originally thought they were. We didn't have the furniture we were used to having, the nice kitchen to cook in, an over abundance of clothing, or an overly nice car to drive. What we did have however, was a bathroom with a hot shower and a toilet, a TV, a computer, and internet access. All things that you don't typically have when you're camping! So, by looking at it as an indoor camping experience, we actually had more than we would've if we were out on our favorite trail in a tent.

When you are going through adversity you have to look at your circumstances through different perspectives to maintain a positive outlook on life, and in some cases, to maintain your sanity.

Spiritual Motivation

I could tell you that I'm such a strong individual that I did all of the things I've mentioned and pulled myself out of financial ruin twice all on my own accord, but that would be the opposite of the truth. I wake up every morning asking for spiritual guidance and I continue to ask for it throughout the day.

For those of you that are "religious" and consider yourselves to be Christian, and went to church with your ex-spouse, and now have to go through feeling uncomfortable or having to find a new church, or anything of that nature I would like to encourage you to have "church" in your own home every day while you are trying to figure those things out.

Some of you may be thinking, "What?!? Not possible, God won't be happy with me unless I show up to an actual building each Sunday!" Well, if you think that, it's probably because you were told that by someone standing in a church at the time they said it. I would like to quote a Bible verse for you that references exactly how God feels about that:

King James Version - Matthew 6:

(5) And when thou prayest, thou shalt not be as the hypocrites are: for they love to pray standing in the synagogues and in the corners of the streets, that they may be seen of men. Verily I say unto you, They have their reward.

(6) But thou, when thou prayest, enter into thy closet, and when thou hast shut thy door, pray to thy Father which is in secret; and they Father which seeth in secret shall reward thee openly.

(7) But when ye pray, use not vain repetitions, as the heathen do: for they think that they shall be heard for their much speaking.

(8) Be not ye therefore like unto them: for your Father knoweth what things ye have need of, before ye ask him.

Translation meaning, lots of people that go to church are hypocrites that go to be seen by others. When you talk to God in secret, he will reward you openly. Talk to him like you're having a one on one conversation with him, don't just repeat things that you've heard other people tell you to say. He knows exactly what you need, he wants to talk to you about it, and he wants to help you.

Now for those of you that just freaked out thinking I'm talking bad about church, if you're still reading, that's not what I'm saying. Trust me when I say, if you're from the South and you consider yourself to be a Christian, then whether or not you show up for church can become a serious issue. My point, is that your spiritual connection to whomever you choose, is a personal issue, not a public display for others to demand of you.

Additionally, if anyone that is religious and also a "Christian" is making you feel guilty about getting divorced you can remind them that the first person that Jesus openly revealed himself as being the Messiah to was a Samaritan woman who had been married five times and was living with a man who was not her husband. This woman was not his same religion or social class, yet he went to Samaria and had one of the most important conversations of his time with her. Back then the fact that he was even speaking to her was abnormal due to their religious and social differences. My point, is that he obviously thought highly of her, and I'm positive that he still thinks highly of you. This can be found in the New Testament; *John 4: 1 – 45.*

My father is Jewish, my mother is traditional Christian, I'm a New Age Christian, my oldest son is named after the Bodhi Tree from Buddhism, and many of the doctors that have saved my son's life are Muslim. I believe that everyone can have an individual personal spiritual connection with whomever they want, and so can you.

I spent four years on an Army base when I was in elementary school and I loved the fact that most of my friends were bi-racial and that they practiced different religions. There are several different religions, but most of them are similar in that there is a good Deity and a dark Deity. The differences between religions is when all of the little details come into play. I knew from the time that I was in 2nd grade that the world is a big amazing place that will be more amazing the more open you are to it.

If your religion makes you feel negative in any way, then find something that makes you feel positive. If you feel like religion is a scary word, then don't focus on religion, focus on spirituality. Like I said before, go take a walk with the trees! Mother nature is an amazing spiritual force that will make you feel wonderful and centered.

In addition to watching the motivational videos I was talking about I also align my chakras every morning, ask Jesus and God exactly what I'm supposed to do that day to be successful, ask my Angels to help me out throughout the day, and I ask my Spirit Guide named David to be sure and get his point across to me all throughout the day. All of that may sound very strange but I do it every day and I've been doing it for many years. I wouldn't be where I am today without all of that help to get me through it. Everywhere I go, and in everything I do, there are seven different entities that help me out. I don't do anything on my own, ever.

Being a New Age Christian for me means that I believe that I made my Life Chart before I even showed up to this realm. Anything "bad" that happens to me was a predetermined test put on my chart by me to test my faith, and all tests were approved by my Messiah, Spiritual Counsel, and God. Therefore, I never say or think, "Why did God let this happen to me?" In my spiritual thought process, there's no such thing.

You can't become a decorated Soldier without going through battles; you can't become a great athlete without being knocked down; you can't have an amazing body without putting in the painful physical assertion required to obtain it; I could go on and on. In the same way, I believe that

I chose specific struggles to go through to test my faith, so that when I get home, I will receive my reward for maintaining my faith through those adversities.

I don't expect any of you to agree with me, I'm simply showing you that I have my own belief process which is shared by very few other people. I am writing a book entitled *The Game* in which I will talk about all of my personal beliefs and how they relate to this thing called life, which I refer to as "The Game".

Very few of my friends and family believe as I do. The only people that think in the way I think are Mediums and I only know they agree with me in some ways because I've read many of their books. I've never met them before, which means I've literally never met another person that has the same belief system as I do. That definitely does not stop me from believing whatever I want to believe, and from having my own daily spiritual routines.

For your own personal spiritual routine, it should start with only yourself and no distractions. As we stated previously, turn off the TV, radio, put down your phone, and just be quiet! Be still and listen. Be still and think about a life that makes you smile. Think about it, then keep thinking about it in more detail. Do this for 30 minutes every morning. That is the best spiritually motivating thing that you could do for yourself. Give time to yourself to think and conceive the best and happiest version of your life.

Manifest Greatness

When you start researching successful people you may hear the term "manifest greatness". What this means, is that you can take actual physical steps to help manifest the thoughts that you've been creating for the happiest version of your life.

You will hear repeatedly that you must first be grateful for everything that you currently have. Like I said before, my son and I were living in one of the most run down apartment complexes in the city, but I sure was grateful for our bathroom, the fact that we were together, that we had our health, the fact that when we stepped out our door we could see Pikes Peak, and for many other things. Writing down the things that you're grateful for on a daily basis will reiterate what you already have to be thankful for, and it will help you to stay positive while you build on new things.

You will also hear the importance of Visualization! The creation of a Vision Board or something visual for you to look at while you're having your motivational time for yourself. You're going to choose things that make you smile, and you're going to put them where you can see them, and you're going to look at them every day and "feel" as though you're in the picture or that you have what the picture shows.

I have a large Vision Board with pictures of my goals hanging on my wall, but before I had that I made a board on my Pinterest app and I saved the vision board pictures I wanted to look at to that board and pulled it up to look at them every day.

I'm 100% nerdy in the fact that I have a dry erase board hanging next to my vision board. It's in three different sections; Conception, In Progress, and Completed. "Conception" is the section for things that I want to do and haven't started actually doing quite yet. "In Progress" is for things that I moved from the "Conception" section and are things that I'm making plans for or have started making progress on figuring out how to obtain those things. "Completed" is obviously for things that I've completed. I like to keep that section up to remind myself of the goals I placed on the board that were achieved. That way I can feel a sense of satisfaction that while many goals are in concept or in progress, I've also achieved goals and that makes me feel a sense of accomplishment.

Remember when I said that achieving goals can become addictive? Well, for me that is absolutely the case. I couldn't imagine a life where I had no goals and nothing to strive for every day. I believe that once you start the process of setting and achieving goals, that you will feel the same way. Empowered!

Being "Selfish"

Your thoughts fuel your actions. Therefore, everything that you have started doing, or will start doing, is extremely important for your success. You have to maintain a positive thought process for these things to flourish in your life. In order for that to happen, you must only surround yourself with positive people, and positive circumstances.

Hmmm, let me guess, most of the people that you know speak in a negative manner on a constant basis. Probably so. As humans we love to have pity parties! Love to throw them, love to attend them, misery loves company and lots of it. No shortage of people that say, "If this person would stop doing this, I could do that", or "I would be more successful if...", on and on and on. As you've learned by this point, you are in control of your own success. As long as you think another person is going to give it to you, you're most likely mistaken.

Every day make it a point to say positive things only! When you are tempted to make a negative statement, DON'T! I want you to think about black confetti flying out of your mouth every time you make a negative statement. Black confetti for the pity party comments, fitting right? When you change how you speak, you will start to notice that other people may have constant streams of black confetti flying out of their mouths. If it's open, well, there it is, flying out with a multitude of negativity behind it.

Sorry ladies, but females in particular, typically like to talk about other people. Be it good, or be it bad, "gossip" has been a centuries long form of communication. And someone asking you how you're doing could unfortunately mean that they're just asking you so that they can turn around and report your pity party specifics to someone else just to have something to talk about.

Successful people don't talk about anything but how to be more successful. This may seem like a strange concept at first, but when you start setting goals and making plans to achieve those goals and someone asks you how you're doing, if you tell them what you're doing, they're probably going to look at you like you're crazy. Your new found craziness is what they're going to report back to others about you. "Yep, Renee thinks that she's going to be able to buy a house because she put a picture of one on a vision board. She can't even afford to go out to lunch anymore, putting a picture of a house on a board is just ridiculous."

When you start to focus on your own success without asking "permission" or requiring the involvement of others, don't be surprised if you get labeled as being "selfish". Merriam-Webster defines **selfish** to mean "concerned excessively or exclusively with oneself: seeking or concentrating on one's own advantage, pleasure, or well-being without regard for others" and also as "arising from concern with one's own welfare or advantage in disregard of others".

I can tell you that those definitions absolutely define who I am, and that the only people's opinions I take into consideration are those of my children. Decisions I make about myself directly affect my children, so I consider those to be one in the same, therefore I suppose "we" are selfish!

When you're going through a traumatic experience everyone will try to be your counselor, your psychologist, your mentor, and so on. If they are giving you positive advice that you like, then great take that in and use it to your advantage. If they are trying to give you advice to conform to the mundane thought processes of the masses, then I would like to encourage you to disregard those comments and focus on being selfish.

My biggest problem with humanity is that we're forced to believe that as adults we have to come in pairs. If you're "single" then there must be something wrong with you, or you "just haven't found that certain someone yet". We go through childhood thinking we can't wait until we're grown, and we won't have someone telling us what to do. Then, we turn around and get into a relationship where the other person does what? Oh, that's right, tells us what to do! Then if we don't do what our partner wants us to do, then we are of course, selfish.

There are no shortage of people that go from one relationship to another with a very short break in between, if any. I call this the "Plug and Play" scenario. One person is taken out of the picture, so you look for another person to immediately plug into their place.

The best thing you can do is stretch out and not focus on plugging in anyone! Enjoy the extra space in your place, in your mind, and in your life in general. For the first time in who knows how long, you don't have someone trying to tell you what to do, or how to think or feel. You're suddenly not responsible for acting exactly as someone wants you to act so that you can maintain their happiness. Enjoy your freedom!

One of the main motivations for people to be a "couple" is to share expenses. As we just covered in this book sharing expenses can cause serious issues when you no longer want to be with that person. I haven't quoted statistics in this book because I'm talking to you personally, so it is irrelevant how many other people are divorced, the focus is on you. However, if we were to look up statistics of how long people can actually stand one another these days, it's not long! Therefore, I believe that whether you are single, or whether you are part of a couple, you must maintain your individuality, and financial independence so that when you are suddenly standing by yourself, your bank account won't notice! Be Selfish friends!

As a hippie and a gypsy, I can tell you that Energy is very real, and that I believe that you shouldn't try to start a new relationship with one person, while the energy of another is still around you. Someone does not have to be standing right next to you for their energy to be on you. Simply thinking about them can cause their energy to affect your moods, your thought processes, and your environment. Give yourself time to clear yourself of any negative energy before trying to bring anyone new into your life. This is not only best for you, but it's best for them as well. This could also take years but giving yourself that time is a priceless opportunity of self-reflection and motivation.

If you feel the need to date, I want you to remember two things that I like to remind myself of. Keep in mind I'm still single because of these things, but I'm also selfish so it works for me:

Compromise = Demise
Compliment = Achievement

The minute you hear someone tell you that you need to "compromise" with them, RUN! Why should you compromise with another human being? With your children, okay, but with a partner, NO! By "compromising" you are giving up a part of yourself. Why would you do that? Most people have compromised for another person to the point that they literally don't know who they are. Compromise rhymes with Demise so always remember that the more you compromise for someone, the more of yourself that you will lose.

Now, if a person says to you that they want to find someone who "compliments" them, then YES! That's what you want! You want someone who compliments you, meaning adds to you, not takes from you. If you can find a partner that will compliment your lifestyle, then excellent because compliment rhymes with achievement and you could possibly achieve great things with that person.

Living in Colorado has inspired the perfect analogy for me. I envision myself rock climbing and I have a specific goal, which of course is to reach the top of the mountain, and next to me, is my partner. Now, we can't share gear, we both have our own harness, and our own rope. To get to the top we literally have to pull our own weight. I can't expect my partner to pull me up, and my partner can't expect me to pull them up. We both have to put in the individual effort to get to the top. We can "compliment" each other and encourage each other, but ultimately, we can't "compromise" our own safety because the other doesn't want to do what it takes to get to the top as individuals.

Two individuals can do great things together when they make the conscious decision to support the needs of one another through the process of complimenting each other.

Patience & Focus

Once you set your plan for success you must have the patience to stick with your goals and not become discouraged as time passes. "Patience" is one thing that most of us have problems with, but it is one of the most important things that you must have and practice daily.

What I would like for you to do, is to go buy a packet of seeds, a little pot, and a small bag of potting soil; total cost will most likely be $10 - $15. Plant the seed and research how to care for it. On a daily basis you will have to check on the seed to look at its progress.

In the beginning, you won't even be able to see any progress because the process will be happening beneath the soil. The seed has to be placed in a dark environment by itself, otherwise the seed won't be activated to become what it is created to be. In addition, the seed must be surrounded by "good soil" that has no negative contaminants, weeds, or rocks. This of course, is an analogy that you can use to relate to your current situation. You must get quiet and plant yourself with the knowledge of what you have the ability to become, and in addition, you can't allow yourself to be surrounded by anything negative that will contaminate your process.

By planting a seed or seeds, you will become more aware that everything has a process. We are spoiled in the sense that we can go to the store and buy flowers that are already in bloom, and vegetables that have already been harvested. Some of us take for granted the fact that those things all started as seeds, and they all had to go through a process to be in their final stage that we are used to seeing and buying.

Always stay focused on what your goal is every day. Plenty of things will try to distract you from the plans that you've put in place, the key is to simply not let them. Stay focused because every day counts. Just as a plant grows every day, you will also grow every day. Enjoy the knowledge that with every minute that passes, you are one step closer to achieving everything you've dreamed of.

Everything in life is a process. Some processes take longer than others, but the main concept is to have patience with the process. If you view your goals and dreams as seeds that you plant, and you care and cultivate them daily, then after the process is complete you will be able to reap the benefits of your harvest.

Conclusion

I hope that by reading this book that it has empowered you to stand as an individual and that is has you excited about what you can do on your own. You are responsible for your own happiness and I hope that I've been able to give you some ideas and tools that help you create a life for yourself that you never thought possible.

My goal in writing this book is to help people that want to take control of their lives to achieve great things, with the main achievement simply being = happiness!

The ultimate goal is to be in a room full of people who've already retained this information and used it to accomplish their dreams. I have already seen a presentation room full of people that stand up as individuals and share their success stories with me and with the others in the room, and with people watching around the world. I hope that you will be one of those people.

www.ingramcontent.com/pod-product-compliance
Lightning Source LLC
Chambersburg PA
CBHW020126130526
44591CB00032B/542